by Janell Glasgow and Ed Shea

Aurora Publishers, Inc.
Nashville, Tennessee

DEDICATION

To those who love life, to the extravagance of the moment, for the escape and joy of a good time. To rogues and ramblers and kindred spirits. To you . . . Laissez les bon temps rouller.

Copyright © 1978 by Janell Glasgow and Ed Shea
All rights reserved.

Manufactured in the United States of America

ISBN 87695-229-5

WELCOME 7	MUSIC AND HIGHLIGHTS
HISTORY 9	OF MUSIC ROW. 57
There's More to Nashville	Milestones in Country Music . . . 59
Than Dolly Parton. 11	Introduction to Music Row. . . . 63
Famous Nashvillians	Highlights of Music Row. 64
and Movements. 13	Annual Music Events 75
Street Scenes 17	How To Get An Autograph. . . . 77
Where To Buy Film 22	WHERE TO EAT 79
MOST OFTEN ASKED	High Brow 81
QUESTIONS 22	Steak and Seafood. 81
TRANSPORTATION. 27	Other Suggestions 83
Car Rentals 28	Some "In" Places 85
Miscellaneous 29	Country Cooking or Soul Food . 86
Airlines 30	Ethnic. 88
Guided Tours 30	Al Fresco. 91
Bargain Airline Fares 31	Vegetarian 92
WHERE TO STAY 33	Delicatessan 92
Our Favorites 33	Not To Be Missed 92
Convenient Locations. 34	Fabulous Fifties 94
Campgrounds 36	Tea Room 94
ATTRACTIONS 41	Abracadabra. 95
Grand Ole Opry 41	Pie Wagons. 97
Opryland, USA 42	In The Countryside 97
How To Get Opry Tickets. 43	Cafeterias and Buffets 99
Country Music Hall of Fame . . . 44	Chains and Fast Food. 99
Tours of the Homes of the Stars. 45	Listings: Where To Find. 99
Dine with Tammy and Dolly . . . 45	Others Open Sunday 100
Webb Pierce Swimming Pool . . . 45	Stars' Kitchens 101
Country Music Wax Museum . . . 46	All-Niters. 101
Feature Sound Studio 46	Good or Great Breakfasts 102
Ryman Auditorium 49	Specialties 102
Hermitage 49	Restaurants by Location. 104
Parthenon 50	How to Pick a Restaurant 105
Upper Room 50	Deadline Additions 106
Tennessee State Museum. 50	NIGHTCLUBS, LISTENING
Tennessee State Capitol 50	ROOMS, BEER TAVERNS. 109
Ft. Nashborough 50	Nightclubs 109
Crow's Nest 51	Disco 111
Belle Meade Mansion 51	Exotic Dancers 111
Governor's Mansion 51	Listening Rooms. 111
Want to Trace Your "Roots"? . . 51	Beer Taverns For Good
Traveller's Rest 52	Ole Boys 113
Cheekwood 52	Bars and Lounges Open
Nashville Sounds Baseball 54	Past Midnight 114
Belle Carol Riverboat Cruise . . . 54	Happy Hour/Cocktails 115
Nashville Speedway 54	Other Night Clubs 115
Hermitage Landing 54	SOUVENIRS 117
Fair Park 54	Trinkets. 117
Children's World 55	Special Reminders. 118
THE HISTORY OF COUNTRY	Christmas Specials. 121

For the Connoisseur. 121	Spring/Summer. 175
MORE TO DO: THEATRE, SYMPHONY, CINEMA, MUSEUMS AND ART GALLERIES 125	Fall/Winter. 181
	WHAT'S LEFT. 185
	News Sources 185
	Favorite Newsstands and Bookstores. 185
Theater and Symphony 125	Beautiful Churches 185
Cinema 126	Tennessee Facts 186
Museums 126	Helpful Phone Numbers 187
Art Galleries. 128	
Gardens and Parks. 130	
Summa Cum Laude — What's Worth Seeing on Nashville's Campuses 133	
Things To Do For Free (And Almost Free) 137	
SHOPPING 143	
Special Shopping Streets and Areas. 144	
Nine Great Boutiques. 144	
Unusual Specialty Shops. 145	
Antiques 145	
Bargains In Them Thar Hills and Where To Find Them 147	
Action Auction. 148	
SIDE TRIPS AND WEEKEND ESCAPES 151	
The Southern Swing. 151	
All Aboard! 153	
The Northern Swing. 155	
Got a Long Weekend? 156	
Short Jaunts. 156	
Presidential Route. 157	
Potpourri Travel Ideas 158	
Civil War Shrines and Battlefields. 160	
One of a Kind. 161	
State Parks. 163	
SPORTS BRIEF: FISHING, GOLF, TENNIS AND MUCH MORE. 167	
Fishing and Boating. 167	
Golf 168	
Tennis. 169	
Horseback Riding 169	
Sailing. 169	
Canoeing 169	
Camping 169	
Hunting. 169	
Rentables. 170	
Spectator Sports 170	
Other Activities. 171	
Grab Bag 172	
ANNUAL EVENTS. 175	

PREFACE

The Good Times Guide to Nashville is a down-to-earth, no-nonsense guide which takes into account simple human limitations: time, energy, money and interest. Since there are literally hundreds of hotels, restaurants, attractions, shops and points of interest in Nashville, we have designed *The Good Times Guide* for the visitor or vacationer or native who wants the most value and enjoyment for his or her leisure time.

We accept no advertising and feel no commitment to exaggerate the attributes nor gloss over the mediocre aspects of any commercial establishment or community organization.

This is a guide which freely admits: Nashville is not perfect. It rains in the winter and spring; it's hot in the summer. Interstate arteries and roads are poorly marked (sometimes immobile), and it is almost impossible to get Grand Ole Opry tickets on the spur of the moment or weeks in advance.

But note: we do not claim to know everything about this city. In fact, anyone who claims so is pretending — if only to himself. There is too much to know, too many anecdotes, too many places and too much that changes before there is time to even share it. (The newest little restaurant open today down the road is closed tomorrow.) So we sought to ferret out the best, the most interesting, while we attempted to avoid the ersatz, the plastic rococo.

Finally, *The Good Times Guide to Nashville* is also a guide for Nashvillians, a compendium of sights to see, things to do and places to explore. We hope it will be used often as an easy reference when the spirit moves you and the lure of a good time beckons. We are hedonists, too.

WELCOME

Nashville is almost 200 years old. It is the gateway to the Sunbelt, capital of Tennessee and home of country music.

Some folks liken it to Hollywood thirty years ago. An inscrutable Mecca for millions of fans and thousands of artists and musicians. Others laud its more genteel reputation as the "Athens of the South," center for 17 institutions for higher learning and the extraordinary Grecian replica of the Parthenon. Still others invoke the living legends of its past, its pioneers and Presidents.

But foremost Nashville is a city of contradiction. It is a "country" town where corporations wheel and deal in riyals and marks and liras. It is a "religious" center where songwriters pen songs about honky tonks. And it is a "manufacturing" crossroads, where Goo-Goo candy bars and Jack Daniel's sippin' whiskey share common ground. It is a collage of bits and pieces woven into an illusion, never too far from images linked to the not-so-distant-past of riverboat wharfs, turn-of-the-century saloons, moonshiners and sharecroppers, one-room school houses, hog killings and trolley cars.

And yet, church spires or honky tonks, Roll Royces or stock cars, Nashville is also a city of beauty and serenity with parks and lakes, tree-lined boulevards and stately old mansions. It rambles over hills and spills into valleys, edges around corners and bumps along the river.

So whether it is the Grand Ole Opry, the Hermitage, Opryland, the Upper Room, Printer's Alley, the Parthenon, Ryman Auditorium, Cheekwood or Belle Meade Mansion, stop and look around. This is Nashville and there's more!

HISTORY

Nashville was founded on Christmas Day in 1779 when James Robertson and a hardy ban of pioneers crossed a frozen Cumberland River. But in prehistoric times, wandering bands of aborigines occupied the territory.

In 1540 Indian villages in the Tennessee River Valley were ransacked by Spainards from Florida; DeSoto, the explorer, left his nation's flag on the bluffs overlooking the Mississippi near Memphis a year later, but more than a century passed before white men entered the area again. In 1710 French traders from Mississippi established a trading post here because of the river location and natural salt lick which attracted animals and could be used to preserve meats. The area in old history books is commonly referred to as "French lick." In fact when Daniel Boone hunted in Tennessee, great herds of bison grazed in the river bottoms, elk and deer inhabited the forest, black bear was plentiful and all manner of game was so rich that it attracted hunting parties of Iroquois from the Great Lakes, Choctaws from the Gulf, and Cherokees from Mississippi. During the summer months Tennessee became the "Land of Peaceful Hunting," a neutral ground where ancient tribal hatreds were forgotten.

Soon bands of pioneers followed Robertson. Small farms sprang up. And these English, German, Scotch, and Irish folk brought with them a vigorous individualism, a set of folk patterns and habits deeply rooted in the remote past. Their music was the old English and Scottish ballad, the fiddle tune and the spiritual. And their culture grew out of their struggle with the earth and land.

Their sons followed Andy Jackson to battle in New Orleans. They listened to Davy Crockett, Tennessee bear hunter and politician, tell his opposition when he was defeated for Congress by a candidate endorsed by Andy Jackson, "You can go to hell, I'm going to Texas." Then some followed him to the Alamo.

Printer's Alley

Yet remember in these days of political cynicism, Nashville's Andrew Jackson was the only President who ever paid off the national debt. And James K. Polk, the first dark horse candidate, was the only politician to fulfill his every campaign promise!

Meanwhile, the Civil War laid claim to some of Nashville's finest men. From 1862 til after the war, Nashville was occupied by Union forces and, although Tennessee was the last state to secede from the Union and the first to return, it was ruled harshly during Reconstruction. (Despite or as a result of having Tennessee's Andrew Johnson in the White House as President.)

But as time passed the wounds healed and Nashville busied itself with going about the business of living. New enterprises were formed, commerce increased and, under the auspices of several churches, new colleges and universities were founded, a legacy Nashvillians enjoy today.

The intervening years passed quickly. Tennessee celebrated its Centennial, the Parthenon was built, Union Station opened its doors, short-story writer O. Henry used Nashville as a setting in "Municipal Report," farmboy Alvin York from Jamestown led seven men to capture 132 prisoners and killed 25 soldiers in the WW I Battle of the Argonne Forest, Prohibition shuttered saloons along Fourth Avenue (driving customers to the rear where speakeasies raged in vogue) and FDR created a new agency, the Tennessee Valley Authority, and lo and behold there were electric lights and air conditioning. Radio and the Grand Ole Opry.

Edgefield in East Nashville was the fashionable side of town (Belle Meade is now) til Tin Lizzies created an exodus to the suburbs. Then this once charmed neighborhood fell victim over the years to fire and tornadoes and indifference. It became a working man's neighborhood cut off from the intellectual and social happenings on the west side of the river. But it remained a bastion for old ward politicians. (Incidentally, Nashville's most recent mayors, Beverly Briley and Richard Fulton, and numerous other public officials have heralded from east of the river.) And today preservationists are attempting to salvage the Victorian homes and cottages there.

But Nashville's history has also included darker moments. There have been cholera outbreaks, train wrecks and floods. Even as late as 1908 Nashville newspaper publisher Edward Carmack was assassinated as he walked along the street downtown. And in 1865, 60 miles south of Nashville in Pulaski, the Ku Klux Klan was founded.

Meanwhile, urban renewal following WW II eradicated the slums and shanties, the infamous "red-light" district, at the foot of the Capitol and old landmarks began to disappear. Nashville became a Metropolitan Government in 1963 and a new building boon emerged in the late 1960's and continued into the 1970's. Today new buildings are under construction throughout Nashville and plans for others are on the drawing board.

But for the most part Nashville has prospered and grown. It has fulfilled the prophecy of Mr. Thomas Bailey, an Englishman and Nashville's first tourist 16 years after its settlement, who observed that Nashvillians were "strong minded . . . capable of carrying on government, becoming wealthy and rapidly improving in education, manners and dress."

Well, Mr. Bailey, if you could just see us now . . .

There's More to Nashville than Dolly Parton

And the Grand Ole Opry and the homes of the stars. In fact, the widely ballyhooed and rhinestone studded $300 million music business is only the 3rd largest industry in town. Printing and insurance are larger.

But the symbols of Nashville's diverse corporate community are more subtle: sleek Lear jets in the hangar, business lunches at the elite Belle Meade Country Club or the exclusive, all-male Cumberland Club and a quiet, social inter-mingling and in-breeding of old guard and noveau riche. (Almost everyone is related to someone in this "brother-in-law town.") But there are no guitar-shaped swimming pools in their backyards, no Nudie suits in their closets.

The city's "Jekyll and Hyde" personality (nothing evil implied) is legendary. For example, would it surprise you to know that Nashville is the home of Genesco, the world's largest apparel manufacturer which once owned Tiffany and now operates Bonwit Teller on Fifth Avenue in New York and Henri Bendel, N.Y.'s chic avant garde shop?

And would you suspect that a Nashville company operates the palatial King Faisal Specialist Hospital and Research Centre in Saudi Arabia? Hospital Corporation of America and its local competitor, Hospital Affiliates International, own or manage more than 150 hospitals in towns and cities across America. Maybe even one in your own hometown.

Then there is National Life Insurance Company, the city's "power broker," owner of WSM radio and TV, the Grand Ole Opry, Opryland and the Opryland Hotel; Cummings Sign Company, the world's largest; the executive offices of Jack Daniel's Distillery; Baird & Ward, printer of "Field & Stream," "Parent," and other magazines; Aladdin Industries, manufacturer of thermos bottles and an array of other diversified products; Capitol Airlines, the world's largest charter airline; Ford Glass Company, the world's largest glass plant; and divisions of DuPont and Avco Aero Structures, and many, many others. But don't forget Standard Candy Company, manufacturer of "Goo-Goo" candy bars.

Meharry Medical College and Vanderbilt University Hospital and Medical School are also important research centers and training ground for doctors and dentists from around the world.

Then, there is a legion of religious operations, companies and concerns in Nashville. In addition to the city's 700 churches, there is the Southern Baptist Convention, the United Methodist Publishing House and the Board of Education, the Baptist Sunday School Board, the national headquarters of Gideons International, the Gospel Music Association, Thomas Nelson Publishers, John

T. Benson Publishing and at least a half dozen denominational colleges and universities, including Belmont, David Lipscomb, Scarritt, Trevecca, Free Will Baptist and Aquinas. In fact, so many religious activities thrive here that Nashville is often referred to as the "Protestant Vatican" of the world.

Belmont Mansion, above; Davy Crockett

Famous Nashvillians and Movements

Can the same city which gave the nation Andrew Jackson give it Pat Boone, Dinah Shore, Rita Coolidge and Brenda Lee?

Nashville has been the birthplace or adopted home to many famous personalities. Many attended college here or were legislators or politicians closely identified with Nashville. They include: Andrew Jackson and James K. Polk, U.S. presidents; Davy Crocket, bear hunter and hero of the Alamo; Sam Houston, Tennessee governor and president of the Republic of Texas; William Driver, coiner of the term "Old Glory" for the American flag; W.E.B. DuBois, founder of the Niagara movement and the first black scholar to receive his Ph.D. from Harvard; Cordell Hull, U.S. Secretary of State and Nobel Peace Prize recipient for his organizational efforts in regards to the United Nations; Robert Penn Warren, novelist; Claire Boothe Luce, writer and U.S. ambassador; Pat Boone, entertainer; Delbert Mann, TV and film producer; Stanford Moore, Nobel Prize winner in chemistry; Dinah Shore, entertainer; Madison Jones, novelist; Guilford Dudley, former ambassador to Denmark; Jesse Stuart, writer; John Hope Franklin, historian; Fred Graham, TV news commentator; Otis Smith, chief legal counsel to General Motors; Phil Harris, entertainer; Clyde Lee, pro basketball player; Eric Lincoln, historian; Wade McCree, Solicitor General of the United States; Bill Inge, author; Nikki Giovanni, poet; George Edmund Haynes, founder of the Urban League; Lou Graham, golfer; David Driskell, artist; James Neal, Hoffa and Watergate prosecutor, and Wilma Rudolph, Olympic gold medalist.

Tennessee Senator Howard Baker and Republican Party chairman Bill Brock also frequently jet in and out of Nashville.

Yet our favorite Nashvillian is William Walker, the "grey-eyed man of destiny." This doctor, lawyer and journalist invaded Mexico in 1853 with 46 men and proclaimed himself President of the Republic of Lower Mexico. Then he led forces into Nicaragua in 1855 and was elected President in 1856. But in an attempt to wage war on Honduras he was captured and executed in September, 1860. Move over Napoleon, this man had vision.

But Nashville has also been the spawning ground for famous movements and legal rulings. Vanderbilt University was the setting for the acclaimed Fugitive movement. Between 1915 and 1928, 16 poets and men of letters at Vanderbilt met to discuss their literary works. Among them were Robert Penn Warren, John Crowe Ransom, Allen Tate and Donald Davidson. They began to publish a magazine of critical comment and verse called "The Fugitive" and created what was to become the Southern literary renaissance.

Later on several members of the Vanderbilt faculty were important spokesmen during the Agrarian movement which advocated the South's return to agriculture as a base for socio-economic prosperity.

And several landmark U.S. Supreme Court decisions have also originated in Nashville's Federal District courts. Baker v. Carr, which broke ground for later decisions involving "one-man-one-vote" or reapportionment, was ruled by the Supreme Court to be a judicial question rather than one of simply politics. Dunn v. Blumstein, which also originated in federal court here, had a nationwide affect on duration of residence for voting purposes. (Vandy Professor James Blumstein initiated this suit.) Then, of course, Tennessee's judicial history is invariably linked to the famous Scopes' "Monkey Trial" and then to the legal wrangling of James Earl Ray, convicted assassin of Martin Luther King, who continues to serve time in the remote Brushy Mountain Prison in East Tennessee.

Point made: there's more to Nashville than Dolly Parton, the Grand Ole Opry, and the Parthenon. Film director Robert Altman tried to capture the spirit of Nashville on celluloid and missed. Who can blame him?

Street Scenes

Nashville is not a walking city, except in certain areas, downtown or Music Row. This earthy, red-flannel and silk-stocking city of 480,000 people covers a 553 sq. mi. area. So a guided tour is the easiest way to become acquainted quickly.

The Good Times Guide recommends our favorite sights in this order: the Grand Ole Opry, Opryland, the Hermitage, Music Row, the Country Music Hall of Fame and Museum, Ryman Auditorium, Lower Broad, Printer's Alley, and Cheekwood. There are tours of the homes of the stars and, considering there are an estimated 750 bona fide millionaires in this town, this is a good way to see how the other half lives!

But to really discover Nashville do take time to explore a few points of interest off the beaten path. Take one of our walking tours downtown.

The Arcade and Tootsie's Orchid Lounge

Begin at Lower Broad where the small shops and *Tootsie's Orchid Lounge* are located then turn the corner on Fifth and there's the old *Ryman Auditorium* — the former home of the Grand Ole Opry before it moved to new quarters at Opryland. Performers between breaks would slip out for a drink at Tootsie's and the nostalgia lingers on in that two block area on either side of Broad. The auditorium is open to the public. Go inside.

Then wander on up to the *First Presbyterian Church* at the corner of Fifth and Church, if it is open, take a look. It is a serene Egyptian oasis right smack in the middle of Nashville. Its dull grey exterior belies the beautiful murals, mosaics and details inside — designed by architect William Strickland whose credits also include the State Capitol and St. Mary's Catholic Church a few blocks away.

Down the block on Fifth (look up as you walk and check the Italinate, turn-of-the-century buildings) is the *Arcade*, a two-tiered 1903 copy of a covered mall in Milan, Italy. The Aracade with its 40 odd shops is an early day predeccessor to contemporary shopping malls. Walk through it, pick up a bag of cashews at the Peanut Shop or an orange at the Fruit Stand, both of which have been in existence as long as most Nashvillians can remember.

Directly across from the Arcade on Fourth Avenue is a series of *Gay Nineties buildings* once centers for gambling and gaiety with names like the Utopia Hotel, Climax Saloon and Southern Turf. When laws changed affecting race track betting and Prohibition came into effect, these establishments closed their front doors and became speakeasies with entry at the rear through famed *Printer's Alley*.

But forget about Printer's Alley for now — until at least the sun goes down. Then it turns into one of Nashville's most popular dining and night club spots. Just remember Andrew Jackson stabled his horses there and walked to his law office.

Amble down Fourth toward Church Street and check out the *United American Bank Building*. The former old Noel Hotel building has been beautifully restored and its crystal chandeliers, brass work and arched windows now gleam. Then glance across the street to the Third National Bank Building. That's where the famous old *Maxwell House Hotel* stood until the landmark burned one Christmas Eve, but the name lives on in the label of the General Foods coffee originally blended and manufactured in Nashville. The company was sold during the 1920's to General Foods for $16 million. It was the coffee that prompted Teddy Roosevelt to say "Good to the last drop!"

Now go back to your car (unless you need some information or assistance from the Chamber of Commerce which is just down the street in the next block) and drive slowly up *Second Avenue*. This is the old warehouse district of Nashville and it is beginning to come back to life as architects, lawyers and businessmen find it a popular business address. The funny, odd building (red brick circa 19th century) on the corner of Second and Broad is the old *Silver Dollar Saloon*, a watering hole for boatsmen and wharf hands years ago. It once had real silver dollars embedded in its floor and bar and is now the home of the Historic Nashville Association.

At the other end of Second Avenue is the Metro Courthouse and Washington Manufacturing Company which makes Dee-Cee jeans and overalls. Back down First Avenue is *Ft. Nashborough*, a replica of Nashville's earliest fort. This entire area is scheduled to undergo a face-lift if the proposed river front renewal comes off as planned. The old warehouse will be turned into a series of boutiques, night clubs and restaurants. But regardless, Lower Broad at the riverfront remains a precious bit of Americana. Feed stores, pawn shops and all!

Tennessee Performing Arts Center under construction

Other points of interest downtown are the *State Capitol*, the *War Memorial and Legislative Plaza*, and the *Tennessee State Museum*. The tall building under construction across from the Plaza is the new *Tennessee Performing Arts Center and Office Complex* and future home of the state museum. Up the street on the corner of Union and Seventh where the Downtowner Motel is located, there is a marker indicating this spot was once the home of James K. Polk and the place where he died of cholera.

Driving back toward Music Row on Broad between Seventh and Eleventh, you'll notice four other Nashville landmarks. The old *Hume Fogg High School* (Dinah Shore graduated from there), the gothic *U.S. Custom House*, *Christ Episcopal Church*, a Victorian gothic building with gargoyles and Tiffany windows, and the beloved *Union Station*, the grey dowager of Broadway which is scheduled to be renovated by the federal government. The Romanesque style building with flying buttresses was dedicated in 1900 and will be turned into a federal office building. It is a magnificent building.

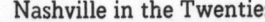
Nashville in the Twenties

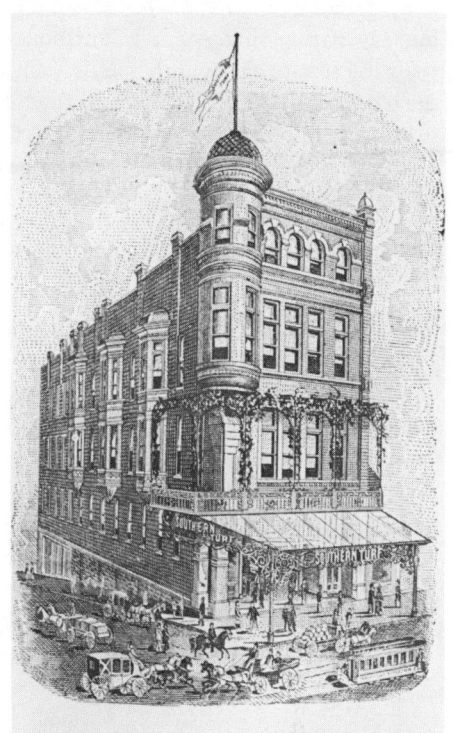

Turn of the century Nashville   SOUTHERN TURF

Footnote: Much of Nashville has changed – just since our childhoods – the Gay Street connector and Courthouse Square renewal demolished some beautiful turn-of-the-century buildings along the river and now only a few remain; the old Andrew Jackson Hotel and the Elks Lodge with its stuffed elk gave way to construction for the Performing Arts Center. And once where there were fields and meadows and even a herd of buffalo, now rises the Opryland complex and miscellaneous campgrounds and amusements.

Where to Buy Film

You may have a cache but if you need some extra film, try Service Merchandise on Lower Broad. This is a catalogue discount store and it usually offers savings on most types of film. Also try Dury's in Green Hills or the Fotomat at the corner of Lyle and West End, not too far from Music Row. Another good place for camera supplies is Grannis Camera Shop at 2115 Hillsboro Drive in Green Hills. There is also film available at most souvenir shops and the Country Music Hall of Fame and Museum.

Most Often Asked Questions

Q. How do I get Grand Ole Opry tickets?
A. Ideally, you should order reserved seat tickets weeks in advance of your visit to Nashville. During the summer the show is sold out for months ahead of time and similarly weeks ahead in the winter.
However, general admission tickets go on sale every Tuesday at the Grand Ole Opry box office prior to the weekend show. Go early, they sell out quickly. See page 43 for complete details.

Q. What are the hours for most attractions?
A. They vary but generally between 8:30 a.m. til 5:30 p.m. There is a tourist summer season in Nashville from June to August when attractions stay open later. For specific hours of individual attractions, see our listings beginning on page 41.

Q. How do I find a hotel room during the peak season?
A. Consider staying at a hotel on the outskirts of town. Or call the Nashville Area Chamber of Commerce Room Finder Service at 244-8080.

Q. What do I wear to the Grand Ole Opry?
A. The name may sound fancy but it is pure casual. Pant suits or skirts and blouses for the ladies. Sport coats or shirt sleeves for the gents. Just remember the Grand Ole Opry house is air conditioned now in the summer so a sweater might be handy, if you chill easily.

Q. What's the lineup for the Grand Ole Opry and when will Dolly Parton or Johnny Cash appear?
A. The lineup is never announced ahead of time til Friday before the weekend performance. Why? Because the Grand Ole Opry officials never know who is going to be in town until that week. The lineup appears in the Friday edition of the morning Tennessean newspaper. And Johnny and Dolly fans are usually disappointed. They rarely appear on the Opry. Johnny is not a member although he does make guest appearances occasionally. And Dolly usually only appears once or twice a year. Why? Again, because they can make more money touring or playing special concerts.

Q. What are the most popular attractions, besides the Grand Ole Opry and Opryland?
A. Music Row (see our highlights on page 64), the Hermitage, the Parthenon, the Upper Room, the Tennessee State Capitol, Belle Meade Mansion, Governor's Residence, Traveller's Rest and Cheekwood. Music Row includes a number of individual attractions, the Country Music Hall of Fame and Museum, the Wax Museum, among others, plus its own special aura. Check our listing of individual attractions, side trips and travel ideas.

Q. Where can I find a restaurant?
A. There are hundreds of eateries in the city. But our guide to local restaurants is the best. It is categorized for easy reference and, since we accept no advertising, we don't exaggerate the quality of the food, service or atmosphere. It includes listings for country cooking, French cuisine, steaks and seafood and much, much more. Listings begin on page 81.

Q. Do all tour services include Grand Ole Opry tickets as part of the package?
A. Some do and some don't. Inquire first!

Q. How do I find souvenirs made in Tennessee (not Taiwan or Hong Kong)?
A. See our complete section on souvenirs on page 117. We feel the same way as you do. So we compiled a list of items indigenous to this area . . . crafts, baskets, Tennessee hams and more!

Q. What is Opryland and is it open year round?
A. Opryland is a theme park. There are rides, restaurants, musical shows,

river front gardens, museums and lots of fun for the entire family. It is really beautifully landscaped. Millions visit it every year. It is also the home of the Grand Ole Opry building. And no, it is not open year round. Just April to November. And only on weekends in the spring and fall.

Q. Where can I hear country music?
A. Don't expect to hear Mel Tillis or Roy Clark or hardly any of the really famous country music entertainers performing locally in lounges or night clubs. (They are usually out on the road touring making lots of money.) But do expect to hear a variety of country music performers, up and coming talent, in the city's bars, lounges and cabarets. See our listing of listening rooms and nightclubs for specifics on page 109.

Q. I can't get Opry tickets, what can I do?
A. Consider the alternatives. The Nashville Jubilee, Ernest Tubb's Midnight Jamboree and investigate what's going on in the local lounges and nightclubs. Check out the listening rooms. And don't forget that television tapings for specials and big name concerts occur frequently. See details on pages 43 & 44.

Q. Where do the stars live?
A. Everywhere. On farms in Williamson County, in residences along Franklin Road, in houses fronting Old Hickory Lake. Take a guided tour of the homes of the stars offered by individual tour companies. There are at least 750 millionaires in Nashville and it is a good change to see how the other half lives! Also see our random directions to the homes of Minnie Pearl, Johnny Cash, Webb Pierce, and Roy Acuff on page 140.

Q. If I have additional questions, who can answer them?
A. The visitors information folks at the Nashville Area Chamber of Commerce at 259-3900 or 244-8500. Or the friendly people at the Tennessee Department of Tourism at 741-2158. The Chamber of Commerce is located at 161 Fourth Ave. N. downtown next to the Life and Casualty Tower; the Tennessee Department of Tourism is headquartered at 505 Fesslers Lane off Interstate I-24 east and both offer a wide selection of brochures.
If you want specific details about attractions, hours, addresses, admissions or more, check the information in *The Good Times Guide to Nashville* first before you call. It may just answer that question for you and save you a dime!

TRANSPORTATION

There are any number of ways to get around this town. There are, of course, the conventional . . . bus, taxi, car rental, and guided tours. But there are also some unconventional, too. By riverboat, limousine and helicopter. For a low price you can even rent a wreck, a dependable used car, pick-up or classic, by the day, week or month! So pick your modus operandi and don't forget that in some areas your feet will be the best method.

PUBLIC TRANSPORTATION

METRO TRANSIT AUTHORITY / 60 Peabody / 242-1662 Provides inter-city and suburban connections. The local bus company also offers service to Opryland, Cheekwood and other points of interest. Check their schedules and destinations.

CAR RENTALS

HERTZ / Metro Airport (361-3131) and Hyatt Regency (256-8123)

AVIS / Metro Airport (361-1838) and 217 7th Ave. N. (255-1234)

BUDGET / Metro Airport (361-4444) and 112 7th Ave. N. (256-2661)

NATIONAL / 10th and Broad (242-8238) and Metro Airport (361-7467)

TAXI

YELLOW / 256-0101
CHECKER / 254-5031
CARROLL / 256-0730

Union Station

MISCELLANEOUS

WRECK RENTERS / 201 4th Ave. S. / 255-8888

LIMOUSINES UNLIMITED / 1631 Lebanon Road / 889-7130

IMPERIAL LIMOUSINES / 1 International Plaza / 361-3055

BELLE CAROL RIVERBOAT COMPANY / 6043 Charlotte Ave. (departure Ft. Nashborough) / 356-4120 or 244-3430

AMTRAK / 1100 Broad / 255-7381 or 800-874-2800

PRIVATE CHARTER AIRCRAFT AVIATION SERVICES / Metro Airport / 361-8070

BIG BROTHERS / Metro Airport / 361-3000

(Check the yellow pages of the telephone book for a complete listing.)

AIRLINES ALLEGHENY / 256-1944
AMERICAN / 244-5500
BRANIFF / 244-4560
DELTA / 244-9860
EASTERN / 244-3780
OZARK / 256-6699
PIEDMONT / 255-8662
SOUTHERN / 242-8381
CAPITOL / (charter only) 244-0230
AIR KENTUCKY / 800-626-1928
NELSON AIRLINES / 361-3559

GUIDED TOURS SOUND CITY / 25 Music Sq. W. / 254-9461
GRAYLINE / 501 Broad / 244-7330
GRAND OLE OPRY / 2800 Opryland Drive / 889-9490
CUSTOM / 1108 Gallatin Road / 227-5200
STAR DUST / 420 Murfreesboro Road / 244-2335
OUR TOWN / Stahlman Bldg. / 242-4560
JOHNNY WALKER / 2400 8th Ave. / 297-8541
GEORGE JONES / 11 Music Circle S. / 259-3993

BUSES GREYHOUND / 200 8th Ave. S. / 256-6141
CONTINENTAL TRAILWAYS / 113 6th Ave. N. / 242-6373

Bargain Airline Fares

Laker Airlines and the Concorde have really revolutionized the airline industry. Subsequently, there are scores of ways to travel in and out of Nashville for almost a pittance. American Airlines offers a Supersaver fare from Nashville to Los Angeles for $203 weekdays. Southern Airlines likewise offers a Fabulous 50 fare from Nashville to Miami for an incredible $94. Braniff, Eastern, Delta, Piedmont, Ozark, Allegheny and others also feature reduced fares. The catch-22 is that there are stipulations and the specials are geared toward slow days for the airlines.

Check with the individual airlines and inquire about their special offers. Or call your travel agent. Stipulations generally include flying after or before a certain time on certain days, booking for a certain length of stay and purchasing the ticket anywhere from seven to 30 days in advance. But in some cases the savings are really worth it! There are scores of cities included in their specials too.

WHERE TO STAY

There are more than 125 hotels and motels in Nashville. If you just want a place to hang your hat, use your own system for picking a spot. Read the billboards or leave it up to fate. ("Henry, just stop at the next motel!")

Our Favorites

OPRYLAND HOTEL / 2800 Opryland Drive / 889-1000

Sumptuous and spacious. Nashville's really first class hotel . . . Las Vegas style entertainment, galleria shops and the works of Tennessee artists brighten its lobby walls. Queen Anne and Chippendale mixed with hunter green decor and oriental rugs create a warm, plush ambiance. Rates begin at $24 for a single room and top out with the Presidential suite. The hotel food is above average, too.

HYATT REGENCY / 623 Union Street / 259-1234

John Portman did well when he designed the first and legendary Hyatt in Atlanta. This is a studied copy of the Peachtree original featuring a high atrium, exposed elevators and revolving rooftop bar. This hotel is also conveniently located downtown across from the Capitol and Legislative Plaza. Cocktails on the second tier is a favorite watering hole for politicians; Hugo's cuisine is excellent and the Blue Max is a good night spot. Food in the coffee shop is fair. No swimming pool. Rates begin at $34 for a single room and top at $48 for a double.

Hyatt Regency

SPENCE MANOR / 11 Music Square E. / 259-4400

Treat yourself to a rare experience if you want to spend a night on Music Row. This ultra-private executive hotel is just a half block from the Country Music Hall of Fame and Museum and a favorite of VIPs. There is no swimming pool or restaurant but ooh-la-la. The 42 suites are beautifully detailed with 24-hour deluxe personalized room service. Complimentary cheeseboard, fresh cut flowers, sauna and courtesy limousine. Rates begin at $50 and top off at $80.

Convenient Locations

MUSIC ROW AND UNIVERSITY AREA

HALL OF FAME MOTOR INN / 1407 Division / 242-1631

This Best Western motel is just around the corner from the Country Music Hall of Fame and Museum. The cocktail lounge is a favorite watering hole for music executives and others. Rates begin at $20 for a single and top off at $32 for a double. Swimming pool.

HOLIDAY INN VANDERBILT / 2613 West End Ave. / 383-1147

Close to Vanderbilt and right across the street from Centennial Park's famed Parthenon. The hotel restaurant offers a good basic bill of fare and Thelma, our favorite waitress, is a globe-trotting jewel! Rates begin at $18.50 for a single and tops off at $32. Swimming pool. Also check out its lounge and entertainment . . . it's usually pretty good.

DOWNTOWN

SHERATON / 920 Broad / 244-0150

A favorite convention hotel downtown. There's also a Sheraton South Inn at Harding Road and I-65 (that's our choice) but it's less convenient to local sights. Swimming pools at both locations. Rates begin at $25 for a single and tops at $38 for a double.

CAPITOL PARK INN / 400 5th Ave. N. / 254-1651

Just a block or two from shopping, Printer's Alley and the Capitol. Swimming pool, bar and restaurant. Rates begin at $11 for a single and tops at $21.50. Also right next door to the Municipal Auditorium.

OPRYLAND . . . Two of the closest!!

FIDDLER'S INN NORTH / Music Valley Drive / 885-1440

Just down the road from Opryland and near Jerry Reed's Nashville Palace. Swimming pool and buffet dining. Rates begin at $8 for a single to $24 for a double.

RODEWAY INN / Music Valley Drive / 889-8235

Again, just right next door to Opryland. Couldn't be more convenient and the Hermitage . . . home of Andrew Jackson . . . is only 15 minutes away! Rates begin at $17 and a double goes for up to $30.

FOOTNOTE: The lack of motel and hotel accommodations in Nashville is a real problem. If our suggested places are booked, ask the desk clerk or reservationist for a recommendation.

UP AND COMING: Three major new hotels are under construction. The *Radisson* downtown and the new *Hilton* at 21st and West End and the *Maxwell House Hotel* at MetroCenter will be welcomed additions. Also, the old *Hermitage Hotel* downtown is being restored and is scheduled to open in the winter of 1979. The old hotel first greeted the public in 1910 and features Beaux Arts design. If renovated true to spirit, it should be a winner.

Campgrounds

HERMITAGE LANDING RESORT / 1001 Bell Road / 889-7050

Sites: 280 (180 with water, electricity and sewer). Rates $7.50 to $12 per day for two persons plus $1 for each extra person. Facilities: pull-through sites, double olympic pool, store, RV supplies, dump station, laundry, shower, ice, recreational facilities, mini golf, fishing, boating, full-service marina, bait shop, gasoline, Nashville sight-seeing tours available from this campground.

NASHVILLE KOA / Music Valley Drive / 889-0282

Sites: 350 (180 with water, electricity and sewer, 150 with water and electricity, 100 with no hookups). Rates: $7.20 to $11 per day for two persons with hookup sites . . . $1.25 for each extra person over 3 years; $1.25 for electric heat or air conditioning. Facilities: Pull-through sites, swimming pool, store, RV supplies, dump station, laundry, shower, LP gas, ice, recreational facilities, bike rentals, TV antenna connection, private phones, babysitters and Opry tickets available in package plan. Tours from campgrounds daily.

TWO RIVERS CAMPGROUND / Music Valley Drive / 883-8559

Sites: 104 (78 with water, electricity and sewer, 26 with water and electricity). Rates: Jan. - May 31 and Sept. 16 - Dec. $7 per day with water, electricity and sewer; $6 water and electricity only. June - Sept. 15 $9.50 per day with water, electricity and sewer, $8.50 water and electricity only. Rates include two persons and children under three, extra persons $1 and $1.25 for air conditioning. Facilities: swimming pool, store, RV supplies, dump station, laundry, shower, ice, recreational facilites, transportation to Opryland and Grand Ole Opry. Tours available from this campground.

HOLIDAY INN TRAV-L-PARK / Music Valley Drive / 889-4225

Sites: 122 with water, electricity and sewer (122 with water and electricity, 100 with no hookups). Rates: $6 - 9 per day for 2 persons; $1.25 for each extra person, $1.25 for electric heat or air conditioning; $1 for sewer. Facilities: all pull-through sites, swimming pool, store, RV supplies, 2 dump stations, laundry, shower, LP gas, ice, game room, miniature golf, shuffleboard, horseshoes, basketball, playground, gasoline, automobile rentals, transportation to Opryland and Grand Ole Opry. Nashville sight-seeing tours from this campground.

FIDDLER'S INN NORTH CAMPGROUND / Music Valley Drive / 885-1440

Sites: 165 (120 with water, electricity and sewer, 45 with water and electricity, 3½ acres with no hookups). Rates: Summer - $6.50 per day and up. Winter - $4 per day. $1 for each extra person, $1 for heater or air conditioner. Facilities: bathhouses, laundrymats, swimming pools, country store, ice cold beverages, RV supplies, patios with picnic tables, dumping stations, pull-through sites, tent sites, playgrounds, restaurants and lounge, miniature golf course.

ATTRACTIONS

PREFACE: Hours change and inflation also occasionally hikes admission fees. Call before you go to make sure attractions are open and check the admission, if that's important to you.

GRAND OLE OPRY / 2800 Opryland Drive / Saturday night shows 6:30 - 9 p.m. and 9:30 - midnight, year round. Friday show: 7:30 - 11 p.m. Jan. 6 - May 26 and Sept. 1 - Dec. 29; June 2 - Aug. 25 Friday shows: 6:30 - 9 p.m. and 9:30 - midnight; Matinee performances: Saturday 3 - 5 p.m. March 25 - Oct. 28; Friday 3 - 5 p.m. June 23 - Aug. 25; Sunday 2 - 4 p.m. June 25 - Aug. 27. Tickets: Reserved $6, General Admission $4, Matinees: Reserved $5, General Admission $3 / 889-3060

If you were born 30 or 40 years ago in Indiana, Ohio, Pennsylvania, Texas or any number of states, Saturday night probably meant listening to the Grand Ole Opry on WSM's 50,000 watt "clear channel 650 on the radio dial." The 2½ hour show began in 1925 as the WSM Barn Dance and today it is the nation's oldest continuous radio program. It is a "must see" whether you like country music or not!! The cast has grown to more than 200 singers, musicians, dancers, and comedians and more than 750,000 faithful fans visit the Opry in person every year. Note: Opry tickets are almost impossible to get on the spur of the moment and since Opry shows are planned on a week-to-week basis, the line-up is announced only a day or so before the weekend show. See boxed details on how to get tickets to the shows and what alternatives there are if you can't!

Grand Ole Opry

Opryland musical and the carousel

OPRYLAND U S A / 2800 Opryland Drive / Season: April 1 - May 28 (weekends only) May 29 - Sept. 8 (open daily) Sept. 9 - Oct. 29 (weekends only) / Admission: Adults (12 and up) $8 Children (4 and up) $7.50 (3 and under free) / 889-6600

Beautifully landscaped and imaginatively designed, this theme park has something for everyone. Restaurants, rides, Broadway extravaganzas, specialty shops and more. The theme is music, music, music and there's fun for the entire family.

How to Get Opry Tickets*

Ideally, you should order reserved seat tickets several weeks in advance of when you plan to visit the Opry, because during the summer the show is sold-out for months ahead of time and similarly weeks ahead in the winter.

But if you arrive in Nashville, four or five days ahead of the weekend show, there is a good chance you might get to see it.

At 9 a.m. every Tuesday prior to the weekend show, general admission tickets, $4 for evening performances and $3 for matinees, go on sale. They sell out quickly and during peak months ticket sales are limited to eight per person. Of the 4,400 seats in the Opry House, 3,000 seats are reserved so the odds are: if you arrive before the box office opens at 9 a.m. Tuesday you will probably get your tickets.

Incidentally, reserved seats are $6 each for evening performances and $5 each for matinees, and can be ordered by mail. Pick up an order form enclosed in the Grand Ole Opry brochure at Opryland or the Nashville Chamber of Commerce.

What to Do If You Can't Get Tickets*

First, make sure there aren't any tickets to matinee performances on Friday, Saturday or Sunday during the summer months. These are not regular Opry shows in that they are not broadcast over WSM radio . . . they are strictly stage productions.

If nothing is available, check out performances which occur on stage in the Opry House every Monday through Thursday during the summer by Opry stars.

The next best and newest alternative to a live performance by a country music entertainer is the Nashville Jubilee, a 2½ hour country music stage show featuring many well-known artists April - October on selected dates at the War Memorial Auditorium. Six to nine acts appear on each show and fans are invited to meander down stage for autographs. Tickets are $5 and $6 for reserved seats. For further information, contact the Nashville Jubilee, Inc. The telephone number is 256-5125.

Then Become a Star Yourself*

Or at least part of the audience for a television taping. "Hee Haw," "Candid Camera," "Pop Goes The Country," "The Porter Waggoner Show" and Johnny Cash specials are just a few of the popular syndicated and network shows taped in Nashville. Check with Opryland Productions and WTVF for details and upcoming schedules.

And Don't Forget*

Almost every bar, cabaret, honky-tonk and saloon features some young talent or aspiring star-to-be. Afterall, Roger Miller, Kris Kristofferson and Waylon Jennings had to start somewhere. And there are also several listening rooms where professional and out-of-town acts appear regularly. See details and specifics under separate heading: Listening Rooms.

And remember that Nashville is a stopping off point in the tours of some of the biggest pop and rock acts in the nation, too. John Denver, Arlo Guthrie, Randy Newman, Barry Manilow, Ferrante & Teicher and even Frank Sinatra have made Nashville a special part of their national tours. The Nashville sound is famous and even the big acts want to say they have played here. (Check the entertainment section of the local newspaper or call Sound Seventy Productions or Lon Varnell for details and upcoming attractions.)

Meanwhile, don't forget about the Ernest Tubb "Midnight Jamboree" which is broadcast live every Saturday night from his record shop over WSM radio. The show is open to the public and admission is free. Top Grande Ole Opry stars perform and it is an unofficial continuation of the Grand Ole Opry. For further details call 255-0589.

COUNTRY MUSIC HALL OF FAME AND MUSEUM / 4 Music Square East /
    Open: Daily September-May 9-5 p.m. June-August 8-8 p.m. / Admission:
    Adults (11 & up) $2 Children (6 & up) $1.50 (under 6 free) / 244-2522

Want to see Elvis Presley's "solid gold" cadillac or the inside of one of those music stars' tour buses? This is the place for you and it is a good place to learn more about the "roots" of country music, too. The popular Nashville attraction also features costumes, instruments, films and is considered a shrine to the stars of country music.

TOURS OF THE HOMES OF THE STARS / see individual listing of tour
   operators under heading: Transportation

Typical tours include the homes of Johnny Cash, Webb Pierce, Minnie Pearl, Eddy Arnold, Kitty Wells, Tom T. Hall, Archie Campbell, Roy Acuff and others. Check our listing of 69 free things-to-do for random directions to several of the homes.

Webb Pierce Swimming Pool   Hall of Fame costumes

Dine with Dolly and Tammy

One of the most popular items on the WDCN-TV annual Action Auction are celebrity dinners with famous country music stars. Held in late April every year, the auction has included extravagant little dinners with Dolly Parton and Tammy Wynette, among others. The dinner with Dolly went for $3,000. (And because the fund-raiser is for public television, non-profit, it's tax-deductible.) And the dinner with Tammy included a balloon ride to an open field, a limousine pick-up, a catered champagne brunch and lots of little classy extras. All for charity . . . Here's to charity!

MUSIC ROW HIGHLIGHTS / See our special detailed section on the famed
   boulevard on page 64.

WEBB PIERCE SWIMMING POOL AND FANS HALL OF FAME / Music
   Square East near the Country Music Hall of Fame and Museum / 9-9 p.m.
   daily / 269-5138

Want your name immortalized on Music Row? Have it inscribed in bronze alongside the edge of the guitar-shaped swimming pool of country music entertainer Webb Pierce. Membership and the one inch engraving is $10 per person. You'll receive a 11 x 14 scroll and membership card. There is an admission to view the pool which is a copy of the one in Webb's backyard.

COUNTRY MUSIC WAX MUSEUM / 118 16th Avenue South / Open: Daily June-August 9-6 p.m., September-May Mon.-Thurs. 9-5:30 p.m., Fri.-Sat. 9-6 p.m., Sun. 9-5 p.m. / Admission: Adults $1.75, Children (6-12) 75 cents (under 5 free) / 256-2490

Authentic costumes, instruments and life-like figures bring 50 of the greatest country music entertainers to life. Mock-sound studio, besides.

FEATURE SOUND STUDIO / 1302 Division / Open: Daily year round 9-5 p.m. / Admission: Adults $2, Children (6-11) $1.25 / 255-0522

Since most folks can't attend a real recording session, this staged production is perfect for those interested in the step-by-step process. Considering most recording sessions can be long, tedious and boring, this is a 40-minute quickie.

Ryman Auditorium

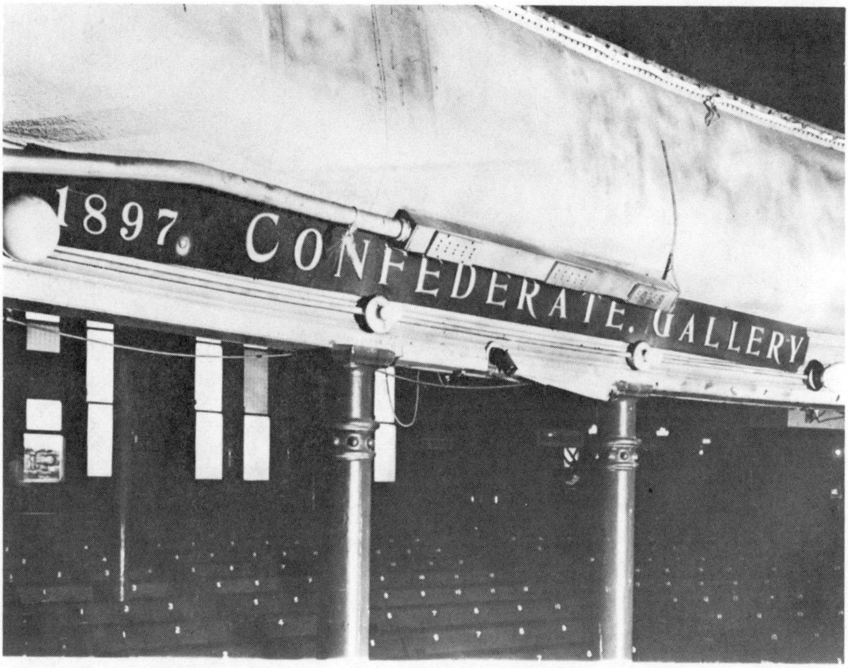
1897. CONFEDERATE. GALLERY

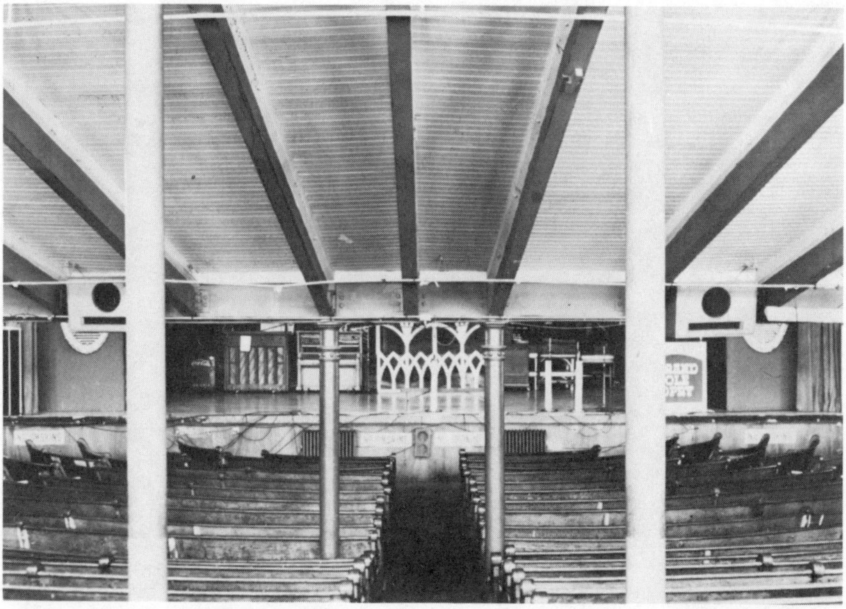

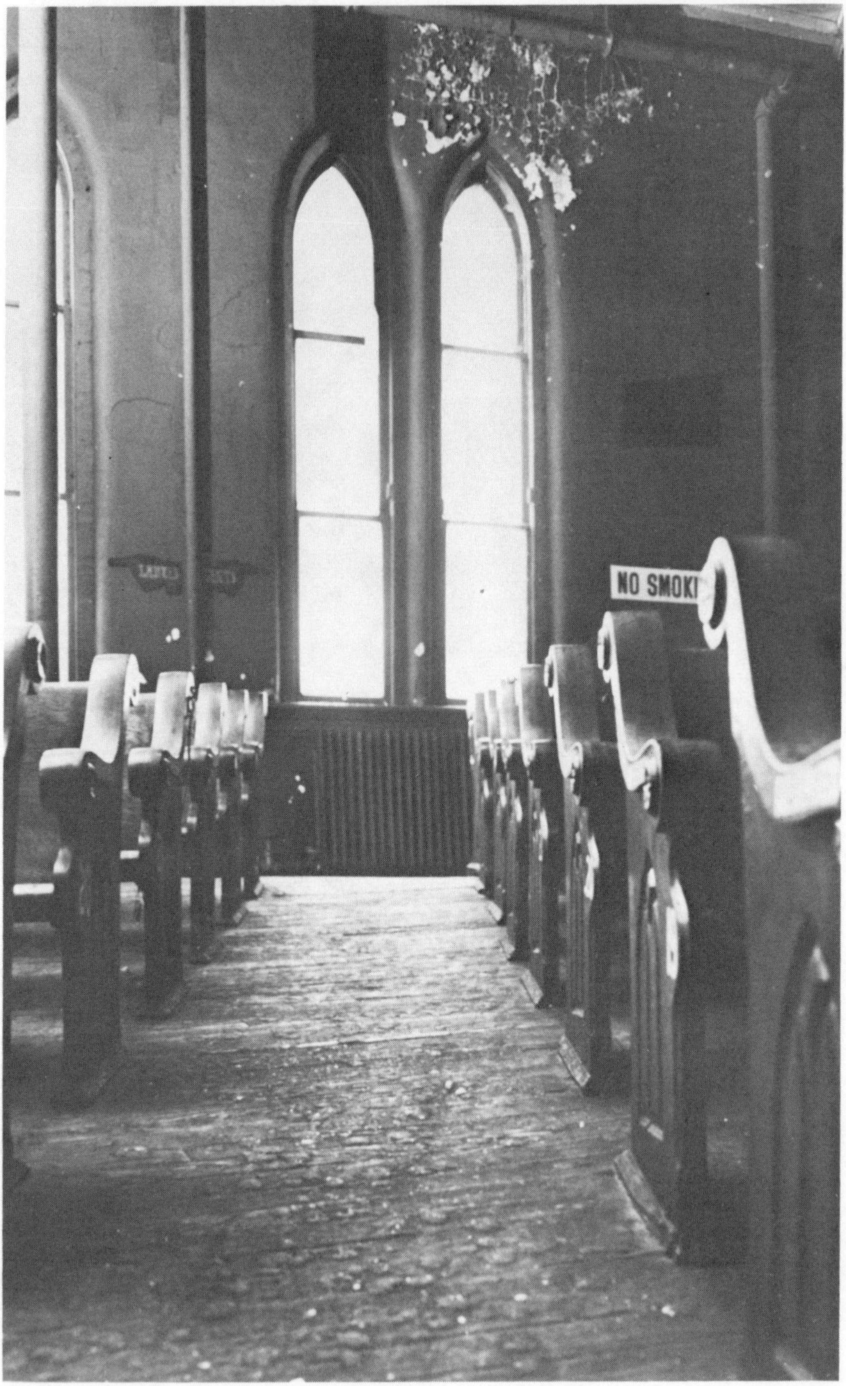
NO SMOKI

Parthenon: Jewel of the Centennial Exposition

RYMAN AUDITORIUM / 116 5th Avenue North / Open: Daily year round 8:30-4:30 p.m. / Admission: $1 / 749-1422

Built in 1891 by riverboat captain Tom Ryman, this was the Gospel Tabernacle and home of the Grand Ole Opry from 1943 to 1974. The old building is now open to the public. Go inside. Step back and look around. Can't you still hear the twang of the guitar, the wail of a heartbreak melody, the sweep of hand fans cooling the faces of an eager audience and then the applause. That's nostalgia!

HERMITAGE / 12 miles east of Nashville on Hwy. 70 N. also access from I-40 / Open: year round 9-5 p.m. / Admission: Adults $2.50, Children (6-13) 75 cents, (under 6 free) / 889-2941

Home of Andrew Jackson. This is one of America's most widely visited historic sites. The mansion and farm are meticulously preserved by the Ladies Hermitage Association and are absolutely beautiful. There are furnishings, personal items, museum and garden. The grounds and house are surrounded by tall magnolia trees and it is cooling and refreshing. What a marvelous break in a sight-seeing routine.

PARTHENON / Centennial Park on West End / Open: Mon.-Sat. 9-4:30 p.m., Sun. 1-4:30 p.m. / Admission: free / 383-6411

No one should miss this sight. Each year more than one million visitors from all 50 states and many foreign countries visit this magnificent replica of the ancient Parthenon of Greece. It is the only replica in the world. The original one in the Acropolis — described as the most perfect building ever erected by man — was destroyed by an explosion in 1687. In 1896 the Parthenon was built for the Tennessee Centennial and it is a reminder of the ingenuity, pride and imagination of Tennessee leaders who wanted to build a monument for generations to enjoy. (During the '96 exposition, all of Centennial Park was a blaze of lights filled with pavillions and pagodas.)

UPPER ROOM / 1908 Grand Avenue / Open: Daily 8-4:30 p.m. / Admission: free / 327-2700

The "Last Supper" wood carving, the Agape gardens and stained glass windows are the highlights of this charming chapel. Peaceful, serene, a favorite stop-off for visitors. The exquisite Persian rugs in its downstairs are real treats, too.

TENNESSEE STATE MUSEUM / War Memorial Building / Open: Daily Mon. & Sun. 1-5 p.m. and Tues.-Sat. 9-5 p.m. / Admission: free / 741-2692

Much of the museum collection is being refurbished and readied for the move across the street to the new Tennessee Performing Arts Center under construction. But there are relics, memorabilia and displays on view including a real Egyptian mummy! So there, King Tut.

TENNESSEE STATE CAPITOL / Downtown on Charlotte Avenue / Open: Daily 8:30-4 p.m. / Admission: free / 741-3211

Take a guided tour of this formal domed building. It stands on the highest hill overlooking Nashville and was built in 1854. During the Civil War it was a federal fortress. There are statues of Alvin York and Andrew Jackson. Architect William Strickland who designed the building is buried within its walls and the tombs of President and Mrs. James K. Polk are also located on the grounds.

FT. NASHBOROUGH / First Avenue near Lower Broadway / Open 9 a.m. to 4 p.m. Mon.-Sat. and Sun. 1-4 p.m. during the summer season / Admission: free / 255-8192

A replica of the original 1780 settlement where "living history" is re-enacted throughout the year. Wearing costumes of the era, guides chop wood, grow vegetables, card, spin and weave wool and make and sell candles and lye soap!

Crow's Nest

Want a panoramic view of Nashville? Try the glass enclosed observation desk atop the Life and Casualty Building — 364 feet up. On a clear day you can see 26 miles. Admission: Adults 35 cents, Children under 12, 25 cents. That's at 4th and Church. Or want to enjoy the view and have a drink? Then saunter on over to the Hyatt Regency Hotel and take a bubble elevator to the Polaris rooftop lounge and restaurant and you'll get a leisurely view of the city and countryside.

BELLE MEADE MANSION / U.S. 70 South / Open: Daily Mon.-Sat. 9-5 p.m., Sun. 1-5 p.m. / Admission: Adults $2, Children 75 cents, (under 6 free) / 352-7350

A restored antebellum mansion once a magnificent estate and a famous thoroughbred horse farm. There's a collection of antique surreys in the carriage house (which is charming, too).

GOVERNOR'S MANSION / 882 South Curtiswood Lane / Open: Tuesdays and Thursdays 1-3 p.m. by appointment / Admission: free / 383-5401

The home of Tennessee's chief executive has 26 rooms and is located on a 10-acre site in an exclusive residential area south of Nashville. The homes of several country music stars are also nearby. Minnie Pearl lives right next door.

Want to Trace Your "Roots"?

Nashville was a frontier destination and point of departure for thousands of pioneers. They crossed the mountains and settled here and then some moved on to Texas and lands west. The Nashville Room of the Main Public Library downtown and the State Archives both have extensive genealogical references and local materials. And the librarians are so helpful.

For archaeology buffs Tennessee is a gold mine. Hundreds of millions of years ago Tennessee was part of a great in-land sea until a series of upheavals drained the sea and left a wide fertile basin rimmed by the Great Smoky, Blue Ridge and Cumberland mountains. Unique geologic formations, caverns and prehistoric Indian mounds are scattered about the state.

TRAVELLER'S REST / off Franklin Road on Farrell Parkway before Brentwood / Open: Mon.-Sat. 9-4 p.m. and Sun. 1-4 p.m. / Admission: Adults $2, Children 50 cents / 832-2962

The historic home of John Overton was a frequent rest stop for travellers during Nashville's early history. Guests included Andrew Jackson, General Lafayette, Sam Houston, and Confederate Generals Nathan Bedford Forrest and John B. Hood.

CHEEKWOOD (TENNESSEE BOTANICAL GARDENS AND FINE ARTS CENTER)/ Cheek Road / Open: Tues.-Sat. 10-5 p.m., Sun. 1-5 p.m. Gardens open til sundown. Closed Mon. / Admission: Adults $2, Children (under 7) free / 356-3306 or 352-5310

Saving the best for last. Like flowers and art? Mansions and museums? This old Georgian mansion is one of the most beautiful in the South and was built by the Cheek family, founders of Cheek-Neal "Maxwell House" Coffee Co. It is the backdrop for 55 acres of flora, fauna and trees. The mansion includes furnishings and a varied art collection — oriental, English portraits, watercolors, contemporary and modern. Cheekwood also hosts major traveling collections such as the Armand Hammer and Chrysler exhibits. Plus special shows by the likes of Gloria Vanderbilt. And every year Cheekwood turns into a glittering fantasy land for the prestigious Swan Ball. Meanwhile, you can enjoy a delicious lunch in the Pineapple Tea Room. (The "Trees of Christmas" each holiday season is another special attraction.)

The Hermitage

Cheekwood

Mixed Bag

NASHVILLE SOUNDS BASEBALL TEAM / Chestnut St., Herschel Greer Stadium / Season: April-September. Game time: 7:45 p.m. / Admission: $1.50-$3.25 / 242-4371

There's a new game in town — Class AA baseball — provided by the Nashville Sounds, a farm team of the Cincinnati Reds in the Southern League.

BELLE CAROL RIVERBOAT CRUISE / Lower Broad at Ft. Nashborough / Schedule: May: daily 10:30 a.m., Fri.-Sun. extra 2:30 p.m. tour, June-August: daily 10:30 & 2:30 except Sun. only at 2:30, September 1-15: daily 2:30 p.m. / Admission: Adults $4, Children $2 / 356-4120

Enjoy Nashville from a totally different perspective. Travel aboard an authentic sternwheeler (which has been the stage for nationally televised specials) and see the scenic Cumberland River, the home of Roy Acuff, Opryland, Demonbreun Cave and more.

NASHVILLE SPEEDWAY / Tennessee State Fairgrounds / Season: April-October every Saturday at 8 p.m. / Admission: $2-$16 / 242-4343

Interested in Nascar sanctioned stock car racing? Motorcycle races and demolition derbys also take place on this 5/8 mile banked track. Home of the Winston 200, Music City 420, Nashville 420 and Marty Robbins World Open 500.

HERMITAGE LANDING / Bell Road / Summer Season: Daily 10-10 p.m. / Admission: Adults $3, Children (under 12) $2 / 889-7050

Palm trees, sandy beaches, Aqua Trak and much more makes this a favorite family spot. Teenagers really enjoy it, too.

FAIR PARK / Tennessee State Fairgrounds / Season: April to September. Open 7 days a week / Admission: free. Rides: 30 cents apiece / 256-6494

A perfect, relatively inexpensive amusement park for the kids. A ferris wheel, merry-go-round and scores of other rides along with concession facilities and more.

Children's World

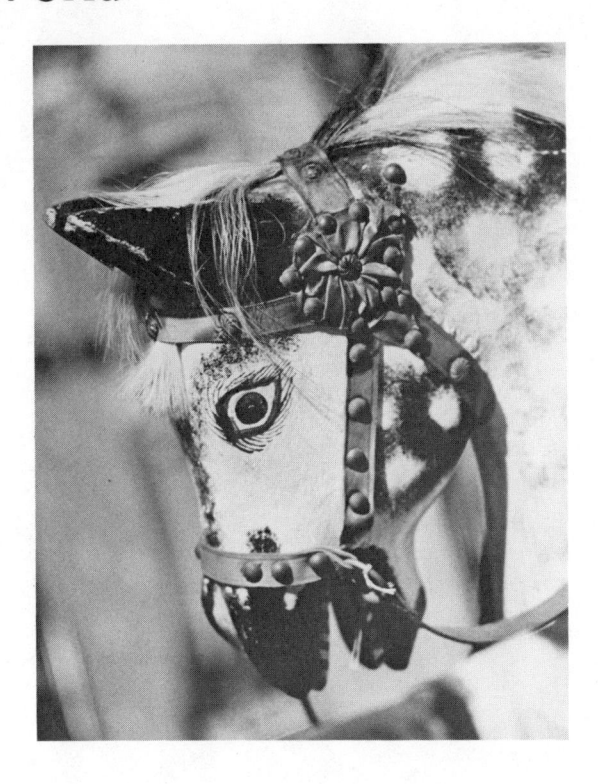

(Ideas for parents facing the third rainy day in a row or the summer refrain . . . "We don't have anything to do!!")

Cumberland Museum * Fair Park * Nashville Public Library * Academy (Children's) Theatre * Tennessee State Museum * Opryland * Centennial Park * Belle Carol Sternwheeler * Municipal Auditorium Skating Rink * Warner Park Riding Stables * Tennessee Game Farm * Ft. Nashborough * Hermitage Landing * Nashville Sounds * the pedal boats in Centennial Park & Shelby lakes.

Specials: Christmas Parade, Barnum & Bailey, Ringling Bros. Circus, Franklin Rodeo, Trees of Christmas at Cheekwood, Bunnyland at Cain Sloan, Captain Ray's Sailmaker Restaurant, Nashville Symphony Christmas Concert and the Ice Capades.

THE HISTORY OF COUNTRY MUSIC AND HIGHLIGHTS OF MUSIC ROW

It has all been said. After all, it has been more than 52 years since Jimmie Rodgers and the Carter family cut a couple of solos in Bristol, Tennessee, and George D. Hay, the "Solemn Ole Judge," quipped something about the Grand Ole Opry over the WSM air waves.

It has been better than 25 years since Hank Williams was found dead in his chauffeured cadillac. And a decade has managed to slip by since "The Johnny Cash Show" and "Hee Haw" premiered on prime time television. The files of the Country Music Foundation, which sprawls below the Country Music Hall of Fame and Museum, groan with the hyperbole and the annotated footnotes. Thousands of clippings, hundreds of articles, scores of reviews, books, theses, (even a Yale University tome) dissect and chronicle the "phenomenon" as it is called.

Rednecks and country music are "in" now. Frye boots, CB radios, Dolly Parton, platinum records, Waylon and Willie, farm living, Jimmy, Rosalynn, Amy and Miz Lillian. And, of course, Brother Billy. But long after the preppies, the politicians and the Beautiful People — all the urban camp followers — move on to another cause célebré (remember Zen, est, Easlen and primal therapy), there'll be the country music fan. The Southerner who remembers.

Out of the poverty, the rural isolation, the hollow and foothill, country music was part of the Southern experience.

In 1969, author Paul Hemphill wrote in the Atlanta Journal-Constitution newspaper: *"Country music was always the exclusive property of the white Southern working class. The intellectual had his Bach. The Negro had his Chuck Berry. The middle age professional had his Glenn Miller. The suburban housewife had her Sinatra. The graduate student had his Brubeck. But the Southern farmer and mechanic and truck drive and route salesman had his Roy Acuff and his Lefty Frizzell and his Hank Williams, and when the steamy Southern Saturday came to an end you could find him mesmerized in front of a radio, the whole family huddled around a big, stand-up Zenith, souls being cleansed, cares being whisked away, spirits being lifted as the glorious sounds of the Grand Ole Opry crackled all the way in from the Ryman Auditorium in Nashville, Tennessee."*

Then Hemphill went on to explain what everyone knows. That "hillbilly" music, as it was once called, was born out of the hardships, toil and isolation of the hill farmer and woodsman. *"It was a scratchy, undisciplined, backwoodsy cacophony of grating fiddles and twanging guitars and singers with head colds,"* he added. *"The stars were country boys a half step off the farm, musicians who couldn't read a lick of music and wouldn't admit it if they could. The arenas were the county fairs and the tent shows and the courthouse squares and the low watt local radio stations of the rural South, radio stations represented by the frantic voices of jakeleg preachers and cure-all elixirs and plastic Jesuses into the night . . . It was the music of the South, by the South, for the South."*

The people. Southerners of yesteryear. They stare at you from the photos. A family album. Dark-haired, dark-skinned, Scotch-Irish men and women, whose ancestors had brought the words and melodies of the Anglo-Celtic songs and ballads from across the ocean 100 years before. They had crossed the Carolina mountains and settled into the Tennessee hill country. They had split rails and plowed fields.

In the background is a garden and rough hewn shack. Three generations: Aunt Maude, corseted and buxom, holding a guitar. Grandmother, a country beauty who bore four children, worked in the field and died at 27 in childbirth with the fifth one. She played the guitar along with the mandolin and bass violin. And father. He sang in the church choir and played the organ. Demographically, they mirror the historical evolution of country music even to the detail that father left the farm, moved to Nashville and worked in a factory. A story repeated a thousand times in towns and hamlets across the South.

Out of the isolation of rural life, the poverty of the agrarian economy, the ravages of war and old prejudices, country music was means of expression, diversion, and amusement for the Southerner who was neglected and cut-off from most educational and cultural opportunities. He held on to his old traditions and kept his music alive. And even when he left the farm, he merely changed the lyrics to reflect his "citified" surroundings.

So, is it only an illusion that a country song sounds better when heard sitting on the front porch or under a shade tree after a dinner of fried chicken, creamed potatoes, sliced tomatoes, boiled corn, snap beans, blackberry cobbler, and iced tea?

And is it so important that the industry today is slick and sophisticated? And does it matter that critics ask: What will happen when the children of those who remember . . . don't want to hear or even understand what a country song represents?

Milestones in Country Music

1920's. The beginning of the "golden age" of country music. The recording industry had ignored the plaintive sounds of country music but broadcasts on radio became popular and talent scouts were sent southward to tap the source. Deford Bailey, a black performer on WSM's Barn Dance, was probably the first country music performer to be recorded in Nashville. Meanwhile, Bob Wills in Texas cornered a following in the late twenties.

1922   WSB radio in Atlanta and WBAP in Ft. Worth sign on the air and feature the earliest known barn dances.

1924   WLS in Chicago follows suit by creating a barn dance segment in its programming at the suggestion of a fellow named George D. Hay, who was later to design programming which included a barn dance format for the new WSM station in Nashville.

1925   WSM radio goes on the air. The new station featured local talent, pianists, sopranos, violinists, orchestral music and appearances by such groups as the Fisk Jubilee Singers. And one lone country music entertainer!

1926   The WSM Barn Dance grows in popularity and George Hay utters something about "Grand Ole Opry" and the name sticks. The entertainment included: Uncle Dave Macon, Deford Bailey, and acts like the Gully Jumpers and Fruit Jar Drinkers.

1927   Jimmie Rodgers and the Carter Family cut a disc for Ralph Peer, an RCA Victor scout, in Bristol, Tn. And the record company is avalanched with mail and requests for their records.

1929   The New York Stock Market crashes. The Depression begins.

1930's. Honky tonks emerged from the depths of the Depression catering to the thirsts and frustration of the laboring man. Jukeboxes evolved as folks sought to find cheaper forms of entertainment. And the music became louder to rise above the din of hell-raising in Southern roadhouses during Prohibition. The lyrics changed, too. No more songs about Mother and religion in that atmosphere. And Hollywood beckoned. Suddenly, there were singing cowboys... Gene Autry, Tex Ritter, Roy Rogers and Bob Wills on the silver screen.

1933　　Jimmie Rodgers dies of TB at the Taft Hotel in New York. Country music loses its first premier performer. But the "Father of Country Music" leaves a following hungry for the sound of the banjo, the guitar and fiddle.

1938　　Roy Acuff joins the Grand Ole Opry and immortalizes hits like "Wabash Cannonball" and "The Great Speckled Bird." He immediately becomes a "star."

1939　　WSM radio gains network status and the crowd on hand to catch the weekly Grand Ole Opry show numbers around 3,000. In July, the Grand Ole Opry moves from the Dixie Tabernacle in East Nashville to the War Memorial Auditorium.

1940's. The turning point in the history of country music. World War II, the transport and intermingling of troops from all parts of the nation and the Armed Forces Network gave country music national exposure. The saga of country music was no longer merely regional in scope. Republic Studio in Hollywood makes a picture about the Grand Ole Opry. Long famous for its instrumentalists, the Grand Ole Opry during the forties becomes equally well known for its array of vocalists.

1940　　Minnie Pearl debuts on the Grand Ole Opry.

1941　　The Grand Ole Opry moves for the fourth time. Now to the Ryman Auditorium, a former gospel tabernacle with church pews and stained glass built by a riverboat captain in the 1800's. Since the program became popular it has moved from the original WSM studio to the Dixie Tabernacle, Hillsboro Theatre and War Memorial Auditorium. Admission is 25 cents.

1942　　The major trade industry publication, Billboard, begins devoting space to articles about country music. And Acuff-Rose (founded by Roy Acuff and Fred Rose) becomes the first exclusively country music publishing house.

1943　　The United States enters World War II.

1945　　Decca begins to record artists in Nashville. Red Foley records in Studio B at WSM.

1947   Ernest Tubb is featured in a concert at Carnegie Hall in New York. He is the first of many country music performers who will play before audiences at the London Palladium, Hollywood Bowl and Madison Square Garden in future years.

1949   Hank Williams records "Lovesick Blues." This spectacular entertainer and writer is to leave an indelible mark on the industry. He bridges the gap between country and popular audiences for the first time with such classics as "Your Cheatin' Heart," "Jambalaya," "I'm So Lonesome I Could Cry," "I Saw the Light" and others. He will be remembered for his talent and his tragic life.

1950's. Rock 'n roll bursts upon the scene and signaled the end of the honky tonk era. Country music executives also realized that country music must change to survive. By the mid-fifties country music radio shows are almost non-existent and the Grand Ole Opry is the undisputed premier show. Kitty Wells becomes the first "Queen of Country Music" and then there's Elvis . . .

1950   The Grand Ole Opry entertainment roster has grown to 120 performers. Capitol Records locates its country director in Nashville. And Patti Page records the "Tennessee Waltz."

1951   WSM radio hosts the first Disc Jockey Convention in Nashville.

1953   Hank Williams dies in the back of his chauffeured limousine en route to a concert on New Year's Day. (The year before he had been fired from the Grand Ole Opry because of his bouts with alcohol and drugs. His marital life, rocky in the past, has been calmed by his second marriage.) He leaves behind his music, his genius, for us to enjoy. Performers like Webb Pierce, Jim Reeves and George Jones will come to fill the the void his death creates.

1954   Elvis Presley signs a recording contract with Sun Records in Memphis. He will record frequently in the years to come in Nashville with RCA.

1955   Tennessee Ernie Ford records "Peace In the Valley."

1956   Rock 'n roll is in full rage. A new galaxy of stars appear: Conway Twitty, Roy Orbison, Jerry Lee Lewis and Buddy Holly. The Grand Ole Opry is briefly televised for two years. And Red Foley hosts the first successful country music television show, the "Ozark Jubilee."

1957   Owen Bradley moves the recording operation of Decca from downtown to 16th Ave. S. The first recording studio on Music Row is a quonset hut.

1958   The Country Music Association is formed.

1960's. The sixties become the growth years in country music. The Nashville Sound becomes famous. It is symbolized by an easy blend of Chet Atkin's guitar and Floyd Cramer's piano. A legion of singers — Loretta Lynn, Tammy Wynette, Dottie West, Jean Shepard and others — vie for the title of "Queen." Honky tonks sounds rebound and Nashville West — Bakersfield, California — produces Merle Haggard and Buck Owens.

1961   Producer Owen Bradley is handling a stable of stars, including Brenda Lee, Connie Francis and others.

1963   Patsy Cline, Cowboy Copas, and Hawkshaw Hawkins are killed in a plane crash. And a year later Jim Reeves dies similarly.

1966   Bob Dylan, the rock guru, records in Nashville.

1967   The first televised Country Music Association Awards show is broadcast. And the Country Music Hall of Fame and Museum opens. First inductees: Jimmie Rodgers, Fred Rose and Hank Williams.

There are now 2,000 radio stations playing country music.

1968   The "Johnny Cash Show" and "Hee Haw" television shows premiere.

1970's. Vietnam has produced a weariness in us all. There's a desire for the simple life, a return to nature. There are Outlaws — Waylon and Willie — and storytellers like Tom T. Hall. Glen Campbell is a perennial favorite and, of course, there is John Denver, Linda Ronstadt, and Charlie Daniels. The sound has changed . . . what's the future?

1971   *Look* magazine features a cover story on country music and

	Kris Kristofferson mugs the cover.
1974	The Grand Ole Opry moves into its new Opry House at Opryland, 10 miles from Nashville. The Ryman Auditorium is empty.
1976	The Grand Ole Opry celebrates its 50th birthday.
1977	Elvis Presley dies at his Graceland mansion in Memphis. And Dolly Parton is interviewed by ABC's Barbara Walters.
1978	President Jimmy Carter hosts a "Country Music Night" at the White House. Country is respectable.

Introduction to Music Row

On a hot summer's day the heat at noon creates wavering pools on the asphalt — mirages — which trick the eye as you drive slowly up the famed boulevard. A Silver Eagle bus is parked on the side street. Inside a recording studio a session which began at 10 a.m. breaks. And upstairs a well-known producer discusses his latest achievement with a couple of executives. Words like bullets, charts, hooks and overdub creep into the conversation.

A few hours earlier a lone troubadour had strummed his guitar as he sat disconsolately at the bus stop bench waiting for his elusive stardom. At 7 a.m. the avenue is trafficked only by early morning commuters who scurry on their way to work. Too engrossed in their own thoughts, they barely notice the encore performance.

"Those who hear not the music think the dancers mad."

It could be Broadway or Sunset and Vine. Only there are no big billboards, no glittering neon lights and no Hollywood sign. Music Row in Nashville is an understated patchquilt of renovated homes and office buildings, punctuated by a few tourist attractions and vacant lots "for sale."

Yet, it is the stage prop for Nashville's $300 million music industry. Here, 5,000 or more people turn up for work every day. At talent agencies, publishing houses and recording studios. Executives, receptionists, musicians, publicists, secretaries and scores of others who help create the "Nashville sound."

Saunter down it. Look around. Beyond the facade of a non-descript clapboard cottage or the polished brass and wood townhome is the creative energy and restlessness of the most famous square mile in Nashville and its remarkable music colony.

(And who knows, maybe you'll run into Chet Atkins, or Ray Stevens. Or one of your favorite stars. That's the best part of Music Row: its element of surprise.)

But even if you don't . . . you'll see for yourself the giant forum where triumphs and failures, hits and misses, old images and kindred spirits come together. It's not idyllic or sun-washed, nor embroidered with spangles, sequins and rhinestones, but it is real! And alive!

Highlights of Music Row

Music Square West

ASCAP / Number 2

This is the oldest and most prestigious performing rights society in the United States. The American Society of Composers, Authors and Publishers was founded more than 60 years ago in New York by the likes of Victor Herbert and John Phillip Sousa. Irving Berlin is a charter member and its roster includes writers Stevie Wonder, Hal David, Neil Diamond and thousand of others. Rory Bourke, Jim Weatherly, Bill Rice, Jerry Foster and Bob Morrison are among its top country writers.
Recent ASCAP country hits include "Feelings," "Don't It Make My Brown Eyes Blue," "You Light Up My Life" and such old favorite standbys as "Caligua," "Mockingbird Hill," "San Antonio Rose," "Delta Dawn," and "Little Green Apples." The interior of ASCAP is beautiful. It is decorated with antiques and an ornate floor to ceiling arched mirror from an Austrian hunting lodge dazzles the eye in the long tabled board room.

TREE INTERNATIONAL / Number 8

The largest country music publishing house in Nashville with operations around the world. The stars in the Tree writer galaxy are as renown as the successes of the company, owned by Jack Stapp and Buddy Killen. It owns much of the catalogue of songwriter and performer Roger Miller, in addition to those of Curley Putnam, Bill Anderson, Hank Cochran, Bobby Braddock and Sonny Throckmorton, among others. Songs penned by Tree writers include "Make the World Go Away," "My Elusive Dreams," "The Green, Green Grass of Home" and many others.

Recent expansions to the Tree building makes it one of the most prominent along the boulevard. Its Spanish motif is also a striking contrast.

LITTLE JIMMY DICKENS and SING ME MUSIC / Number 19

This "office" complex is typical of the way many old cottages and homes have been renovated. Large rooms are subdivided and paneled. Barn siding is a popular remodeling material. The low monthly overhead for this type of office space has created headaches for leasing agents of the sophisticated high-rise buildings down the way.

STUDIO B / Adjoining the RCA Building

Elvis Presley, Charley Pride, Jim Reeves, Perry Como, Al Hirt, Waylon Jennings and many others have recorded here in this famous studio owned by RCA and now operated by the Country Music Hall of Fame and Museum. It is open to the public and demonstrations and explanations are provided by guides. Admission: Adults $1

NASHVILLE SONGWRITERS ASSOCIATION / Number 25

1000 members from the unknown and unpublished to the legendary — Loretta Lynn, John Denver, Kris Kristofferson, Willie Nelson and Bill Anderson — belong to this international society. Inside hang wonderful charcoal sketches of the great songwriters of our time, Hank Williams, Gene Autry, Bill Monroe, Mel Tillis, Vaughan Horton and Merle Haggard, among others. All part of the Songwriters Hall of Fame.

R C A / Number 30

Ronnie Milsap, Tom T. Hall, Jerry Reed, Jim Ed Brown and Helen Cornelius, Waylon Jennings and Dolly Parton are among a few of the stars who record on the RCA label.

Chet Atkins, "Mr. Guitar," is head of the creative operations and Jerry Bradley, son of Owen Bradley (who started the Music Row phenonmena in 1957 by setting up a recording studio in a quonset hut at 804 16th Ave. S.), manages the other half of this famous Music Row landmark.

APRIL BLACKWOOD / Number 31

This is the publishing arm of CBS headed by Music Row's Charlie Monk. Among its writers are Bill Rice and Jerry Foster, the most prolific chart-busting team in the industry.

GOSPEL MUSIC ASSOCIATION / Number 38

Nashville's "bible belt" environs make this association's location a natural. And companies like John T. Benson, Word Music's Nashville operation and entertainers like Bill Gaither are sure fire catalysts. Many in this music town predict a bright future for this growing industry. The GMA Dove Awards are scheduled to be televised henceforth. And GMA is planning to build new quarters, a Hall of Fame nearby.

WARNER BROTHERS MUSIC / Number 44

This half of the Warner Brothers operation administers the Eagles catalogue.

Incidentally, according to local lore, this renovated office building was once the apartment house Kristofferson lived in when he was a struggling young songwriter. Rent: $25 a month. He worked as a bartender around the corner at the now defunct Country Corner tavern to help pay for it. Times do change.

A T V / Number 45

This operation owns much of the famous Beatles catalogue. (Not to mention "Lucille.") Enough said.

FORMERLY THE FOUR STAR BUILDING / Number 49

This buidling has gone through hard times. It ended up in receivership; its name was ripped off the front and a man fell to his death from the atrium penthouse level late one night. The original owner was a visionary (but tight money and finances strapped a dream). It is now the headquarters for several concerns including the office of Record World, a major industry trade publication.

UNITED ARTIST TOWER / Number 50

Recently acquired by EMI of Europe, UA is representative of the appeal large international conglomerates see in the entertainment industry. Local producer Larry Butler has moved on to independent status producing Johnny Cash, Kenny Rogers, Dottie West and Charlie Rich, among others. The West coast headquartered label continues to record many of those, in addition to Billie Joe Spears and Crystal Gale.

BUCKHORN MUSIC / 1007 17th Avenue South

This operation of Marijohn Wilkins, owner, includes several early Kristofferson pieces. She was a believer when he was a janitor.

ADVENT THEATRE / 1202 17th Avenue South

Nashville's newest professional theatre in this old remodeled Episcopal Church. Its productions run the gamut from tragedies to comedies.

G. HILL AND COMPANY / 1206 17th Avenue South

Television, movies and jingles comprise an important segment of the local industry. Gayle Hill and company have produced numerous jingles for companies like Coke and others. Remember "Country Sunshine"?

Music Square East (16th Avenue South)

CEDARWOOD / Number 39

One of Nashville's oldest publishing houses. Founded by Bill Denny, Sr., his son now heads the operation. The James Denny Artists Bureau was one of the biggest booking agencies in Nashville during the early 1960's.

CAPITOL / Number 38

Anne Murray, James Tally, Freddie Hart, Billy "Crash" Craddock, Asleep At The Wheel, and Glen Campbell are among those who record here. Capitol was the first West coast concern to locate here.

COMBINE / Number 35

Bob Beckham, a "songwriter's publisher," is the chief honcho here. Tony Joe White, Larry Gatlin, Billy Swann, Kris Kristofferson and others write for this pop publishing house. Monument Recording's Fred Foster is part owner here, too.

COLUMBIA / Number 34

Billy Sherrill, Nashville's most talented and successful producer/writer, is really the star here. Tammy Wynette and Tanya Tucker, among others, have been groomed by Sherrill. Lynn Anderson records here also.

The building itself is built around the original quonset hut Owen Bradley used when he began the Music Row phenomenon here in 1957 by recording such folk as Brenda Lee, Conway Twitty and Loretta Lynn. Bradley is credited with moving the embryonic recording industry from downtown to Music Row.

M C A / Number 27

Tanya Tucker, Nat Stuckey and Hoyt Axton are among others who record on this label. Formerly Decca.

MONUMENT / Number 21

A major locally-owned recording company (most of the recording studios are owned by West coast concerns), which produces Larry Gatlin, Tony Joe White and Eddy Raven. Fred Foster owns this studio.

SPENCE MANOR HOTEL / Number 11

Nashville's ultra private and plush motel for VIPs. No restaurant, just 24-hour personalized room service. Beautiful suites, sauna, limousine, fresh cut flowers and your own chef. Not bad, eh? Several Nashville corporations rent these suites by the year.

WEBB PIERCE SWIMMING POOL AND HALL OF FAME
    FOR FANS / Located between the Music Sqaure Park
    and the Spence Manor Motel

This guitar shaped swimming pool, Music Row's newest tourist attraction, is a bonafide copy of the one in Webb's backyard. For $10 per person, a fan can have his name inscribed in bronze along the edge of the pool and become immortalized for posterity — the way country music greats have left their mark on the sidewalks leading to the Country Music Hall of Fame (only they contributed $1,000 for the honor) Grauman's Chinese Theatre style.

BROADCAST MUSIC INCORPORATED / Number 10

This performing rights corporation and the Country Music Hall of Fame next door have been likened by author Paul Hemphill to the twin spires of the Mother Church . . . or was it archangels? Regardless, BMI is a Music Row fixture and so is executive director Frances Preston. (She goes back to the time when country music was scorned by most folks.) Cool and professional, she even pre-dates women's lib.

The building itself reflects the Preston personality. Sophisticated. Grey velvet covers the walls in her office and fades into a grey carpet. Lots of plants and open spaces. (The board room features a trompe l'oeil effect of clouds and cherubs floating aloft in pastel shades on the ceiling.)

COUNTRY MUSIC HALL OF FAME AND MUSEUM / Number 4

Inside is Elvis Presley's "gold" cadillac, a genuine tour bus, costumes and displays. And a very nice gift shop. A must see!

Side Streets Along The Boulevard

GRAND AVENUE

WARNER BROTHERS RECORDS / Number 1706

Emmylou Harris, T. G. Sheppard, Rex Allen, Jr., Sandy Posey and Donna Fargo are among those who record on the Warner label.

AHAB MUSIC / Number 1707

This is Ray Stevens studio and office. Nice, quiet and subdued.

SOUND LAB / Number 1708

One of many private recording studios scattered throughout the area.

QUADRAPHONIC / Number 1802

Buffy St. Marie, Joaz Baez, Paul Williams, Jimmy Buffett and Leonard Cohen are just a few of the folks who have recorded here.

18TH AVENUE SOUTH

PARAGON HOUSE / Number 803

Gary Paxton and gospel music entertainer Bill Gaither, among others, work out of this office.

PETE DRAKE'S / Number 809

Another local spot where jingles are cut for radio and television commercials.

OWEPAR / Number 813

Dolly fans . . . this is the publishing house for the blonde bombshell who happens to be one of the industry's most prolific writers and greatest entertainers. Dolly Parton. And right around the corner is Fireside Publishing. Owned by none other than Porter Waggoner himself.

SINGLETREE / Number 815

Formerly owned by the singing cowboy Gene Autry. It is now owned by David Burgess.

19th Avenue South

GLASER RECORDING / Number 916

The Glaser Brothers own this fine studio and the copyright to one of the classic country melodies . . . "Gentle On My Mind."

CANAANLAND / WORD MUSIC / Number 825

Word Music's Nashville division operates from this office. The Waco, Texas, concern is probably the largest gospel music publisher. The local operation is headed by Aaron Brown.

MUSIC CITY RECORDERS / Number 821

Beatles' Ringo Starr and the Duke, John Wayne, have both recorded here!

MUSIC CIRCLE SOUTH

U. S. RECORDING / Number 12

Ronnie Milsap recently acquired this recording studio. It has been one of his ambitions to own his own private studio. And now it's realized.

SESAC BUILDING / Number 11

This is the third performing rights society with a location in Nashville. Jim Black heads up SESAC. The privately owned New York corporation always throws the ritziest party during the annual DJ convention held here every October.

POLYGRAM/MERCURY / Number 10

Faron Young and Jacky Ward record on the Mercury label. Henry Hurt and Jerry Kennedy head up this internationally famous music company.

JOE TALBOT AND ASSOCIATES / Number 2

Joe Talbot is a leading industry spokesman. He is a very nice man who owns one of the major record pressing companies in town. The Nashville office of Cashbox, one of three major weekly trade publications, is also headquartered in this buidling.

MUSIC CIRCLE NORTH

COUNTRY MUSIC ASSOCIATION / Number 7

It bills itself as the most "active trade organization" around. Executive director Jo Walker has been at its helm since the inception. She is soft spoken and politically astute and under her leadership the association has grown and grown.

Coal Miner's Daughter Music, Loretta Lynn's publishing company, also leases space in the CMA building along with others.

FEDERATION OF MUSICIANS / Number 11

These music-making folks are really the ones responsible for the Nashville Sound — that improvised, loose and easy melody we all love!

DIVISION STREET

FARON YOUNG BUILDING / Number 1300

This office building includes a number of tenants, among them . . . the Association of Country Entertainers, sponsors of the "Nashville Jubilee;" "Music City News," a local trade paper; Playboy Records and Frank Sinatra's Frank and Nancy Music.

SOUND SHOP / Number 1307

This top recording studio is owned by Tree publisher Buddy Killen.

ELSEWHERE — OFF MUSIC ROW

ABC DOT / 2409 21st Ave. S.

Jim Fogelsong heads up this local operation. The Oak Ridge Boys, Jimmy Buffett and Don Williams are among those who record on this label.

JACK CLEMENT STUDIO / 3102 Belmont Blvd.

Cowboy Clement is famous and this recording studio bears his name. It was once a Camelot for young writers and producers who could learn and experiment with their creative energies.

HOUSE OF CASH / Nashville Pike / Hendersonville

This is the House that Cash built. Johnny Cash lives just down the lane from this recording studio. It is a long ways out but a nice drive.

JIM REEVES ENTERPRISES / Madison

This is another music operation which escaped the hustle of Music Row. Mary Reeves Davis, widow of Jim Reeves, continues to administer his catalogue of great hits.

ACUFF-ROSE / 2510 Franklin Road

Roy Acuff and the late Fred Rose, along with the great Hank Williams, created this legendary publishing house. Wesley Rose continues to oversee this operation. It was the first exclusively country music publishing house in Nashville.

On the Drawing Board

BILLBOARD MAGAZINE . . . is planning to build a major office building on the land between Division and Laurel Avenue. It will house their radio station activities as well as their publishing concerns.

GOSPEL MUSIC HALL OF FAME . . . money is being raised to build the proposed shrine to be located across the street from the Country Music Hall of Fame and Museum. Nashville's strong religious heritage reinforces GMA's growth and long-range goals.

Annual Music Events

CHARLIE DANIELS VOLUNTEER JAM / Held annually in January at the Municipal Auditorium. Call Sound Seventy for details and date.

OPRYLAND OPENS / The first weekend after Easter. All kinds of musical entertainment. Open only on weekends til the summer months.

NASHVILLE JUBILEE / A series of special concerts, sponsored by the Association of Country Entertainers, at the War Memorial Auditorium beginning in April through October on selected dates.

FAN FAIR / A fantastic extravaganza for the hard-core country music fan. A week-long round of shows, autographs, sessions and performances usually held the first or second week in June. Attendance around 15,000 persons from all over the nation. Call the Country Music Association for details.

NASHVILLE SYMPHONY SUMMER CONCERTS / Begins the last of May at the bandshell in Centennial Park on selected Sunday afternoons. Call the Metro Park Board or the Nashville Symphony for the summer schedule.

OLD TIME FIDDLER'S JAMBOREE / Held annually in Smithville, Tn., in late June or early July. Contact the Dekalb County Chamber of Commerce for details.

UNIVERSITY OF THE SOUTH SUMMER CONCERTS / Usually begins in July on various Sunday afternoons. Call the university for details or check the newspaper listings.

"DOWN TO EARTH" ALL-DAY SING / An old-fashioned all-day, dinner-on-the-ground gospel sing in Alexandria, Tn., in mid-July.

NASHVILLE SYMPHONY FALL CONCERT SERIES / The regular symphony season begins in September. Call the Nashville Symphony for details.

GRAND OLE OPRY DJ CONVENTION / Staged early or mid-October. There are private parties, galas, shows and the nationally televised Country Music Awards presentation.

GOSPEL MUSIC DOVE AWARDS / The industry annual awards held in early November. Call the Gospel Music Association for details.

FANNIE BATTLE DAY CAROLERS / An old Nashville tradition. To raise money during the Christmas season for the Fannie Battle Day Home for Children. Always in December.

Fiddling Jamboree at Smithville and Opryland

Note: Writer's nights at various clubs, such as the Exit In; Ernest Tubb's Midnight Jamboree, special appearances by touring groups and artists, as well as televised tapings are always a part of the Nashville music scene. Watch the newspapers for announcements and listings.

How to Get an Autograph

Ask for it, first. If you see your favorite star, don't be shy. When the day comes that no one asks for his or her autograph, that's when it is going to hurt!

The "Nashville Jubilee," staged at the War Memorial during the summer, encourages the fans to come down stage for autographs. And although there is a lot of milling about on the Grand Ole Opry stage, don't expect to be able to obtain an autograph unless you know someone back stage. But after the Opry, the Ernest Tubb Record Shop holds a "Midnight Jamboree" at the record shop store and you might be able to corral a star there. Of course, if you are lucky you might run into your favorite star on Music Row during the day or at one of the nearby restaurants frequented by the music industry crowd . . . O'Charley's, Ireland's or Hap Townes.

Then of course you can always request the autograph by mail by addressing it to the individual star's office or recording company. (The Music Row zip code is 37203; check our highlights of Music Row for additional details.) And don't forget, Webb Pierce makes routine appearances at his tourist attraction on Music Row.

WHERE TO EAT

This is the best part of the book! Why? Because we, the authors, get to recall all the good times we've enjoyed at these spots. The funky lunches, the home cooked meals, the elegant little dinners.

We have deliberately omitted the non-descript, the neon purveyors of heartburn and indigestion, the places we have frequented and tried to forget.

Because we realize you may not have time to take in all of the following, if you are a visitor, may we recommend a few of the following from varied categories? For the high brow: Julian's, Hugo's, Elliston Hall, and the Brass Rail. For a bit of the orient: the Dynasty. For the best steak and salad bar: the Peddler. For the greatest variety of fresh seafood: the New Orleans Manor and the Shack. For downtown lunch: Satsuma, Langford's and Candyland. For the "in" places: Houston's, Friday's or Spats. For country cooking: White Cottage and Belle Meade Motel. For the best breakfast: Loveless Motel Restaurant. For one-of-a-kind: Elliston Soda Shop and the Gerst House.

Still not what you are looking for? Then read on. All-niters, cafeterias, ethnic, fast food, Sunday brunch, unusual settings, kitchens of the stars and more.

To the Nashvillian, we suggest you try them all! There are more than 75 restaurants listed here under headings which reflect the diversity and imagination of the hundreds of eateries operating in Nashville. We have been to all of them at one time or another. And we hope you will, too, in the course of time.

But please — do call before you go. Restaurants come and go in Nashville, and hours change in even the most established restaurants.

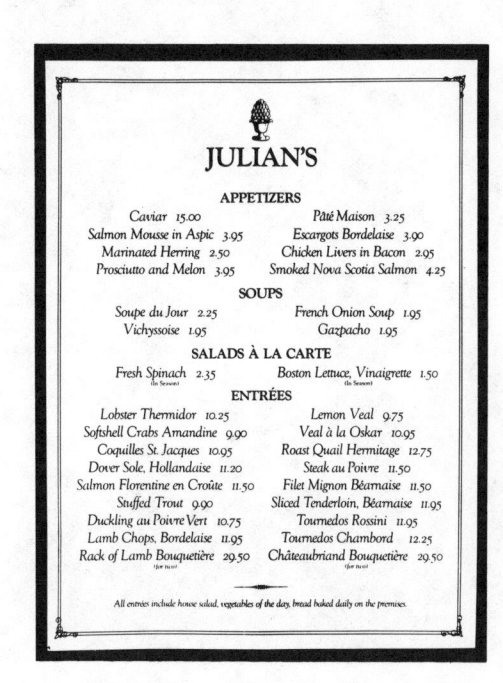

JULIAN'S

APPETIZERS

Caviar 15.00	Pâté Maison 3.25
Salmon Mousse in Aspic 3.95	Escargots Bordelaise 3.90
Marinated Herring 2.50	Chicken Livers in Bacon 2.95
Prosciutto and Melon 3.95	Smoked Nova Scotia Salmon 4.25

SOUPS

Soupe du Jour 2.25	French Onion Soup 1.95
Vichyssoise 1.95	Gazpacho 1.95

SALADS À LA CARTE

Fresh Spinach 2.35	Boston Lettuce, Vinaigrette 1.50
(In Season)	(In Season)

ENTRÉES

Lobster Thermidor 10.25	Lemon Veal 9.75
Softshell Crabs Amandine 9.90	Veal à la Oskar 10.95
Coquilles St. Jacques 10.95	Roast Quail Hermitage 12.75
Dover Sole, Hollandaise 11.20	Steak au Poivre 11.50
Salmon Florentine en Croûte 11.50	Filet Mignon Béarnaise 11.50
Stuffed Trout 9.90	Sliced Tenderloin, Béarnaise 11.95
Duckling au Poivre Vert 10.75	Tournedos Rossini 11.95
Lamb Chops, Bordelaise 11.95	Tournedos Chambord 12.25
Rack of Lamb Bouquetière 29.50	Châteaubriand Bouquetière 29.50
(for two)	(for two)

All entrées include house salad, vegetables of the day, bread baked daily on the premises.

New Orleans Seafood Fe

High Brow

JULIAN'S / 2412 West End / Dinner Mon.-Sat. 6-10:45 p.m. / 327-2412

Reliably sophisticated. Its wine list and French cuisine is Nashville's best. The townhome atmosphere is elegant. Dover sole, lemon veal and duckling au poivre vert are a few of the specialties. Nashville's only four-star restaurant. Reservations recommended.

HUGO'S / Hyatt Regency Hotel / 623 Union Street / Dinner 6-9 p.m. 7 days a week / 259-1234

Superb dining. Again, one of Nashville's finest. American cuisine and a pampered atmostphere. Good service.

BRASS RAIL / 206½ Printer's Alley / Dinner Mon.-Sat. 5-midnight, Closed Sunday / 254-1218

Steaks, lobster tails, prime ribs and one of the nicest wine lists in town. Entertainment nightly. It is very much a "man's" restaurant. Lots of portraits of Jackson and a nice burnished ambiance here. Excellent service.

DYNASTY / 3415 West End Avenue / Lunch and dinner 7 days a week, lunch 11:30-2:30 p.m., dinner 5-10 p.m. / 269-0188

Restaurants come and go in Nashville and here's hoping this one is around for a long, long time. Serving the finest in Peking and Szechuan style cuisine and reasonably priced in an elegant setting.

Steak and Seafood

PEDDLER / 3 locations: 110 Lyle Avenue (327-2325), 4243 Lebanon Road (889-1780) and 903 Gallatin Road (865-6314) / Lunch 11-2 p.m. (Lyle & Lebanon Rd. only) Dinner 5:30-11 p.m. Mon.-Sat., Sun. 5-10 p.m.

Steak lover? This is Nirvana. It also features the best salad bar in town. You buy your steak by the ounce (8 oz. minimum) at your table. What more could you ask for?

FIFTH QUARTER / 295 Thompson Lane / Lunch 11-2 p.m., Dinner 5-11 p.m. til 12 Fri-Sat.; 7 days a week, Sun. 4-10 p.m. / 242-3583

Pleasant dining. Steak and prime rib is the speciality. A great salad bar. Good lounge and entertainment.

APPETIZERS

101	Egg Rolls (2)	1.50
102	Bar-B-Que Spare Ribs (4)	2.95
103	Bar-B-Que Pork	2.50
104	Templa Shrimp (4)	2.95
105	Shrimp Balls (4)	2.95
106	Fried Wonton (4)	1.50
107	Pop-Pop Beef (4)	2.50
108	Shrimp Toast (2)	1.75
109	Flaming Plate	4.50
	(assorted tidbits for two)	
	(2.00 for each additional portion)	

SOUPS

201	Wonton Soup	餛飩湯	1.00
202	Egg Flower Soup	蛋花湯	.75
203	† Hot and Sour Soup	酸辣湯	1.25
204	Sizzling Golden Rice Soup (for two)	鍋巴湯	2.95
	(1.50 for each additional portion)		
207	War Wonton (for 2 or 3)	餛飩湯	3.50
	(fresh made wonton with shrimp, beef, and chicken)		

Additional Soups in Chef's Specialty

A la Carte Dinners are served with tea and one portion of rice.
Each additional serving of rice is .40

RICE AND NOODLES

301	Peking Fried Rice	北平炒飯	3.95
	(Mandarin style fried rice with chicken, beef, shrimp, and green peas)		
302	Shrimp Fried Rice	蝦炒飯	4.50
303	Beef Fried Rice	牛肉炒飯	3.95
304	Ham or Bar-B-Que Fried Rice	火腿炒飯	3.95
305	Fried Rice or Plain Rice	飯	.40
	(serves one)		
306	Mandarin Chef Noodles	什錦炒麵	4.95
	(soft noodles with beef, shrimp, pork, chicken and vegetables)		
307	Chinese Fried Noodles	兩面黃	5.95
	(both sides golden-the most fancy and tasty pan-fried form to serve)		

VEGETABLES

401	Buddhist Delight	炒素什錦	4.95
	(mixed sauted vegetables)		
402	Broccoli Saute		4.50
	(broccoli with bamboo shoots)		
403	Sweet and Sour Vegetables	糖醋白菜	4.50
	(Chinese Bai-Choy with sweet and sour sauce)		
404	Sauted Snow Peas and Water Chestnuts	青豆馬蹄	4.95
405	Winter Flavors	冬菇豌豆	5.50
	(Chinese mushrooms and snow peas)		
406	† Ma Po's Bean Curd	麻婆豆腐	4.50
	(bean curd with spicy minced meat)		

† *Spicy and Hot*

SEAFOOD

501	Stir-Fried Shrimp with Peas	青豆蝦仁	7.50
502	Peking Crab	炒蟹肉	8.95
	(crab meat with straw mushrooms, bamboo shoots, and water chestnuts in special sauce)		
503	† Lobster Mandarin	干燒龍蝦	9.95
	(Lobster tail meat with mushrooms, bamboo shoots, and water chestnuts in special sauce)		
504	Lobster Cantonese	廣東龍蝦	9.95
	(Lobster tail meat in traditional Cantonese style)		
505	Shrimp with Glutinous Rice Cake	蝦仁鍋巴	8.95
	(shrimp in tomato sauce served with sizzling rice)		
506	Shrimp with Lobster Sauce	蝦蓉湖	7.50
507	† Shrimp with Hot Ginger Sauce	干燒明蝦	8.50
	(shrimp with yellow onion in spicy tomato sauce)		
508	† Kang-Pao Shrimp	宮保蝦	8.50
	(deep fried shrimp with spicy sauce and water chestnuts)		
509	Sweet and Sour Shrimp	甜酸蝦	7.50
	(deep fried shrimp with sweet and sour sauce)		

Additional Seafood Dishes in Chef's Specialty

JIMMY KELLY'S / 4310 Harding Road / Dinner Mon.-Sat. 5:30 til midnight / No credit cards / 292-3090

A favorite Nashville steak place for more than 40 years. Loose and mellow, reminiscent of a speakeasy. Also features seafood and Southern style foods.

NEW ORLEANS MANOR AND SEAFOOD FEAST / 1366 Murfreesboro Road / Dinner, Tues.-Sat. 6-10 p.m., Closed Sun. & Mon. / 367-2777

Take one old antebellum mansion. Fill its entry hall with two long tables of the greatest variety of seafood in Nashville and voilá! It is one of the best new restaurants in town. Clams, crab legs, oysters, chowders, herring, salmon and much more. All you can eat for $15.95. Salad bar. Steak or lobster as the main course. Fresh strawberries and melons for dessert. Sumptuous!

THE SHACK / 2420 Gallatin Road / Seven days a week from 11:30 a.m. til 10 p.m. / 859-9935

Throw your peanut shells on the floor, Jimmy C. This non-chalant spot way out on Gallatin Road serves beer and live Maine lobster, Florida stone crabs, peel-and-eat shrimp, catfish and more. Good fish and an easy, informal atmosphere. Try it!

CAPTAIN PAULO'S / 1601 Riverside Drive / Lunch and Dinner: 11-8 p.m., Fri. & Sat. til 9 p.m. Closed Sun. / 227-7482

Hush puppies, fried catfish, boiled shrimp and a fisherman's catch is the specialty of this little hole in the wall restaurant in East Nashville. But it has cornered its share of the celebrity market. Liza Minnelli has dined there! It is funky and good.

Other Suggestions

SPERRY'S / 5109 Harding Road / Dinner 5:30 - 11 p.m. Mon.-Thurs., til midnight Fri. & Sat., til 10 Sun. / 353-0809

Candlelights, burnished decor and English tudor design sets the mood for good steaks, crab legs, escargot, lobster and more. This is a very popular place and features a good lounge — very clubby. No entertainment.

ELLISTON HALL / 217 Louise Avenue / Tues.-Sun. Dinner 6-11 p.m., Sunday brunch 11-2 p.m., Closed Monday / 327-0302

Drawing rooms, fireplaces and a distinctive flair has the odds makers betting this newer dining spot might turn into a winner. Intimate and carefully detailed service. Specialties: Beef Wellington, duck, lamb, prime rib and more. Very good.

SMUGGLER'S INN / 1204 Murfreesboro Road / Lunch 11:30-4 p.m. Dinner 5-11 p.m. Mon.-Thurs., til midnight Fri.-Sat., Sun., 5-11 p.m. / 361-4440

Got "Saturday Night Fever" and wanna dance? And want some good food? This lively place features steaks and seafood. It is popular with the young crowd and seems to attract those who like good food, too.

O'Charley's

O'CHARLEY'S / 402 21st Avenue South / Lunch 11-2:30 p.m., Dinner 5-10 p.m., til 11 p.m. Fri.-Sat., Brunch 11-2:30 p.m. Sat. & Sun. / 327-3773

A lunchtime favorite of Music Row executives because of its location, decor and terrific looking waitresses. The food is good, too. Hamburgers, steaks, and spaghetti are the specialties. Fresh cut flowers decorate the tables and bunches can be bought at the door. Evening dining is also very pleasant. Very good service. One of Nashville's best established restaurants.

MARIO'S / 1915 West End Avenue / Dinner 5:30 p.m. to 11 p.m. Mon.-Sat. / 327-3232

Want to see a celebrity? Or can't decide what you want — maybe something Italian or just steak? Try Mario's. He is very special.

JUDY WEST'S / 31 White Bridge Road / Lunch 11-3 p.m., Dinner 6-midnight, Lounge 11-2 a.m., Closed Sunday / 352-7482

Like piano bar entertainment? Steaks and prime ribs? This informal spot is a popular place.

Some "In" Places

HOUSTON'S / 3000 West End Avenue / Lunch and Dinner 11-midnight Sun.-Thurs., til 1 a.m. Fri. & Sat. / 269-3481

The quiche is the best in town and the salads are great. Pleasant atmosphere: brick archways, lots of plants and wood, ceiling fans and good service. One of the most popular spots in town.

FRIDAY'S / 2214 Elliston Place / Lunch and Dinner Mon.-Sun. 11:30-2 a.m., Sunday brunch 11:30-2 p.m. / 329-9575

The classic. Indescribable and great if you don't mind confusion and humanity. The decor is eclectic, nostalgic and zany. But the food is good and the appetizers sensational. Fried mushrooms, peel-and-eat shrimp, hamburgers and fries, etc. The menu runs on page after page graffiti style. Try it. (N.Y.'s greatest contribution to Music City!)

SHENANIGAN'S / 3324 West End / Lunch and Dinner 11-11 p.m. Mon.-Sun. / 298-4470

Sit in front in a big bow window, sip chilled white wine, and enjoy. This renovated old house has taken on new life and is an "in" place for sandwiches, steaks and salads.

BISHOP'S CORNER / 3201 West End / Lunch and Dinner 11 a.m. - midnight 7 days a week til 1 a.m. Fri. & Sat. and til 10 Sun. / 383-9288

A cozy little corner built around a blazing fireplace. Sounds good? It is. Omelets, steaks and sandwiches are the specialties. (Try their avocadoes stuffed with crabmeat, too.)

Spats

SPATS / 1601 21st Avenue South / Lunch and Dinner 7 days a week 11 a.m. til / 320-7130

This is our favorite close to Music Row. The specialty is barbecued ribs and, next to the Rendezvous in Memphis, the best in Tennessee. Easy atmosphere and just a terrific place for a drink and a snack. (The word is also that they are opening one on Nolensville Road, so watch for it. The Lipman brothers also have Spats restaurants in Birmingham and Louisville.)

Country Cooking or "Soul Food"
(no credit cards accepted)

WHITE COTTAGE / 1102 3rd Avenue North / Lunch only 11 to 2 p.m. / 251-9120

This tiny restaurant at the foot of the Jefferson Street Bridge is one of a kind. Almost perfection. Fresh vegetables, delicious desserts, homemade rolls and down home hospitality. Go early for lunch — they sell out fast!

White Cottage

BELLE MEADE MOTEL RESTAURANT / 5133 Harding Road / Breakfast, lunch and dinner 6 a.m. - 10 p.m. / 352-2317

Its fried chicken, corn, steak and biscuits, turnip greens and potato salad are legendary. What more could you want?

LOVELESS MOTEL RESTAURANT / Highway 100 South / Breakfast 8-11 a.m. Lunch 11-2 p.m. Dinner 5-9 p.m. Tues.-Sun. Closed Monday / 646-9700

It's way down the road on Highway 100 but it is worth every mile driven. A small cafe serving the best country ham, fried chicken and biscuits around. The biscuits and fresh jellies and jams just melt in your mouth. Sensational!

HAP TOWNES / 493 Humphries / Lunch only 11-3 p.m. Mon.-Fri. / 251-9648

Chet Atkins sometimes lunches here. And Hap Townes is a rare breed: a darn good cook and a mighty fine art collector. He'll serve you himself from behind the counter. Good country cooking in a small setting.

SYLVAN PARK / 4502 Murphy Road / Lunch and Dinner 10:30-7 p.m. Mon.-Sat. / 292-9275

Watch for it or you'll drive right by it. Why is it the best country cooking is served in small spots? Almost unnoticed, undetected. You have to ferret them out like jack rabbits (or "sift" for them like Klondike gold). This is another jewel. Try it. Parking is hopeless but the food is mighty good.

BUDDIE'S / 406 12th Avenue South / Breakfast, lunch and dinner 6 a.m. - 7 p.m. Mon.-Fri. / 256-7016

Very close to Music Row. Good country cooking in a real cozy place. Harnesses, gourds and other country items decorate the walls. And there's a great jukebox.

Ethnic

German

GERST HOUSE / 228 Woodland Street / Lunch and Dinner 11-10:30 p.m. Closed Sunday / No credit cards / 256-9760

Picture a Munich beer hall, slightly gaudy, but filled with a special nostalgia. This restaurant is a Nashville landmark and may it never change. The oyster roll is out of this world, the beer is great and, well, the apple strudel is one of a kind. Go. Try it.

Chinese

PEKING / 1923 Division / Dinner 5-10 p.m. Mon.-Thurs., til 11 p.m. Fri. & Sat., Closed Sunday / 327-1083

A red lacquered rickshaw and authentic decor greets the diner who will enjoy Mandarin cuisine here. Close to Vanderbilt and Music Row. Good and very relaxing.

KOBE STEAKS / 210 25th Avenue North / Dinner 5-10:30 p.m. Mon.-Thurs., til 11:30 weekends / 327-9081

Japanese cuisine served in authentic style and setting. Dinner is prepared at your table. This spot has received high ratings.

INTERNATIONAL MARKET AND RESTAURANT / 2010-B Belmont Blvd. / Lunch and Dinner, daily 10:30-7:30 p.m., til 8 p.m. Sat. / 297-4453

Ever walk into a restauant and just know that it is going to be different? That's the International Market. It is a marvelous schizophrenic little hole in the wall catering to the worldly epicurean (dried Korean fish, Manischweitz matzo balls, woks, etc.) and other intrepids sorts. Good oriental fare served seven days a week on one side of the market from the steam table.

International Market and Restaurant

Italian

VILLA ROMANO / 2007 Terrace Place / Dinner 7 days a week 4 p.m. til midnight / 327-2185

The food is delicious and the old turn-of-the century house is an architectural gem. The drawing rooms have been turned into formal dining areas . . . maybe just a bit too formal. But this place is a must if you love Italian food. Tableside serving and preparation.

CIRACO'S / 212 21st Avenue South / Lunch 11-2 p.m. Mon.-Fri., Dinner 5 p.m. til midnight 7 days a week / 329-0036

There are two sides to this restaurant: a bright pizza nook and then a cozy candlelight lounge and restaurant. Pizza by the slice and a full and varied Italian restaurant fare. Just across the street from Vanderbilt University.

CARMEN'S / 5404 Harding Road / Lunch and Dinner 11-11 p.m. Sun.-Thurs., til midnight Fri. & Sat. / 352-3621

This is a good family spot. Pizza, lasagna and more. It also serves beer, wine and cocktails.

Mexican

MISSISSIPPI WHISKERS / 1713 Church Street / Dinner only / 320-9118

Not your typical gringo Mex-Tex joint. Very good Mexican food in a rustic setting. Nightly entertainment.

LA FIESTA / 436 Murfreesboro Road / Lunch and dinner Mon.-Sat. 10-10 p.m., til 11 p.m. Fri. & Sat., Closed Sunday / 255-0539

Traditional Mexican specialties. Tacos, enchiladas, refried beans and more in a colorful decor.

Spanish

VISCAYA / 1907 West End Avenue / Lunch 11-1:30 p.m. Mon.-Fri., Dinner 5-11 p.m. Mon.-Sun. / 327-0487

There's only one Spanish restaurant in town and that's the Viscaya. The food is delicious and the sangria is perfection. The black bean soup is great and so are the paellas.

Polynesian

BLUE HAWAII / 81 White Bridge Road / Mon.-Sun. Lunch 11-2 p.m., Dinner 2:30-10:30 p.m., til 11:30 weekends, Sat. & Sun. buffet / 356-1110

Diamond Head is just around the corner. Sweet and sour pork, egg flower soup, etc. American cuisine is also served. Sit in one of those giant fan rattan chairs and play Truman Capote in Tahiti.

Indian

MAHARAJAH / 3307 West End Avenue / Dinner 5:30-10 p.m. Sun.-Thurs., til 11 p.m. Fri. & Sat. / 292-9143

Discover the tastes and moods of India. Kebobs, curries and other authentic specialties. Also sells Indian spices, brass and leatherworks.

Al Fresco

MAUDE'S COURTYARD / 1911 Broadway / Lunch 11-2 p.m. Mon.-Sat., Dinner 5:30-11 p.m. Mon.-Thurs., til midnight Fri. & Sat., Brunch Sunday 11:30-2 p.m. / 320-0543

One of Nashville's newest. A rustic courtyard gives way to shades of Williamsburg decor inside. Varied menu leans toward seafood and lighter fare. (All the right ingredients should make this spot a winner.)

Maude's Courtyard

HOUSTON'S / 300 West End Avenue / 11-11 p.m. / 269-3481

Gaily striped umbrellas beckon you from the side at one of Nashville's most popular "in" spots.

Vegetarian

LAUGHING MAN / 1926 Division / Breakfast 7-10 a.m., Lunch and dinner 11-9 p.m., Sunday brunch / 320-9071

Here's to your health. Steamed vegies, smoothies, breads, sandwiches and desserts are all natural. As their ad says: 100% natural, 100% Nashville.

Delicatessen

MORRIS ZAGER / 221 6th Avenue North (255-3108) or 3813 Hillsboro Road (385-3995) / Downtown: 8:30-6 p.m. Mon.-Fri. and Sat. 8:30-4:30 p.m., Green Hills: 10-6 p.m. Mon.-Fri. and Sat. 10-5:30 p.m.

The downtown location is our favorite. The Jack Special is great — hot corned beef and melted cheese on rye, big sliced pickles. A super spot for lunch and breakfast is also served. Good Kosher foods and condiments. At one time this old eatery featured a men's balcony and some of the old wood paneling and arched mirrors have been moved to this more spacious location on 6th Ave. Also bakery goods sold at both locations.

Not to Be Missed

SATSUMA TEA ROOM / 417 Union Street / Lunch only 10:45-2 p.m. Mon.-Fri. / 256-0760

Light and refreshingly delicious. This charming eatery is Nashville's oldest restaurant in operation. Arrive early for lunch to avoid the crowd and enjoy soups, salads, fresh vegetables, homemade rolls and incredible desserts including ice creams made fresh that morning. Mmm-good.

ELLISTON PLACE SODA SHOP / 2111 Elliston Place / Breakfast, lunch and dinner 6 a.m. til 9 p.m. Mon.-Sat. / 327-1090

Flip the calendar back and revel in this 1940-ish soda shop. Chrome bar stools, black and white tiles, juke boxes, red neon sign and the best sodas, malted milks, and concoctions in town. Also try their country cooking. The owners also operate the Sylvan Park cafe.

Elliston Place Soda Shop

CANDYLAND / 631 Church (256-5946) and 2916 West End (383-4164) /
  Lunch and snacks 10:30-6 p.m. (West End) and 10:30-3 p.m. (Church Street) Mon.-Sat.

Our favorite location is the downtown shop on Church Street. Try their chicken salad sandwiches and ice creams, sodas and sundaes. This place doesn't change — it is a Nashville landmark. Old booths, faded sherbert decor and quaint ice cream parlor tables for two.

ROTIER'S / 2413 Elliston Place / Lunch and Dinner 9-11:45 p.m. Mon.-Sat. / 327-9872

A favorite of Vanderbilt students for years. It serves a great hamburger. Order a beer and play the pinball machine.

Fabulous Fifties

LANGFORD'S / Life and Casualty Tower at 401 Church Street / Lunch and coffee shop 6:45 a.m. til 3:30 p.m. Mon.-Fri. / 256-1626

Nothing has changed here, the decor is still 1950'ish. But the food is good. Try the Faucon salad — a Nashville original named after Monsieur Faucon and his turn-of-the-century restaurant. Very good. Also tasty sandwiches, great raisin rolls and well-seasoned vegetables.

HARVEY DEPARTMENT STORE'S FOUNTAIN DINETTE / Basement of Harvey's 518 Church Street / 9-4 p.m. Mon.-Sat. / 254-9511

A favorite of downtown shoppers. A good place to stop and enjoy a soda or sandwich. It has been around for a very long time. The apple pie a la mode is our favorite.

CAIN SLOAN DEPARTMENT STORE'S IRIS ROOM / Cain Sloan's 501 Church Street Store / Lunch 11-3 p.m. Mon.-Sat., Dinner til 7:30 p.m. Mon. & Fri. / 255-4651

Again, another place for shoppers and folks downtown. It was once a very proper place for ladies before women's lib made shopping unfashionable. Ah, those days of taffeta and white gloves . . . Good food.

Tea Room

PINEAPPLE ROOM / Cheekwood (Tennessee Botanical Gardens and Fine Arts Center) at Cheek Road / Lunch only Tues.-Sat. 11-2 p.m. / 352-4859

Enjoy a leisurely lunch here. A perfect proper setting in this historic mansion. Tour the grounds and view the art. Satisfying and pleasant.

Abracadabra

(Unusual Settings)

CAPTAIN RAY'S SAILMAKER / 4243 Harding Road / Lunch 11-2 p.m., Dinner 5-11 p.m., til midnight Sat. and 5-10 p.m. Sun. / 298-2645

Cast ahoy! This extraordinary restaurant is the most lavishly decorated in Nashville. Designed to recreate seafaring adventures and story book fantasies. Steak and seafood are the specialties. Visit the Polynesian lounge. Comic heroes and heroines will be your waitresses and waiters.

DELI JUNCTION / 2000 West End Avenue / Mon.-Thurs. 10-10 p.m., Weekends 11-midnight / 242-2795

Take a train and turn it into a deli. Decorate it with gingham curtains, cedar planks, plants and install a side room, glass enclosed, for lunchers and deli aficionadoes.

JUDGE'S CHAMBER / 206 Public Square / Mon.-Fri. 5:30 a.m. til 7:30 p.m. / 254-6789

Save an old turn-of-the-century warehouse sitting on the courthouse square. Feature home cooked food, serve breakfast, lunch and dinner. And specialize in call-in and take-out orders. That's what this place does.

SCHMEISER'S GREAT AMERICAN MUSIC HALL AND DINING SALOON / 631 2nd Avenue South / Lunch and Dinner 11-2 p.m. and 4:30-3 a.m. Mon.-Sun. / 255-2131

Small tables now grace the amphitheater where doctors taught students the mysteries of life in this building once the Medical School of the University of Nashville. This old structure is being restored, the food is fair, the service slow but it gives you time to absorb the atmosphere.

MAPLE FOX / 142 2nd Avenue, Franklin / Tues.-Sun. lunch 11-2 p.m. Dinner 5:30-9 p.m., Closed Monday / 790-1350

"Here's the church and here's the steeple, open the door and here's the people." This old church turned restaurant is one of Franklin's charming little spots. Lunch fare is open sandwiches, salads and casseroles. Dinner hearty entrees, prime rib, chicken and more.

BELLE CAROL RIVERBOAT DINNER CRUISE / 6043 Charlotte Ave. (depart Ft. Nashborough at Lower Broad) / Twilight cruise 6-8 p.m. and moonlight cruise 8:30-10:30 p.m. / Season: June-August, Weekends: March, April, May, September, October and November (Groups anytime) / By reservations only / 356-4120

Take a twilight or moonlit dinner cruise along the Cumberland River aboard the Belle Carol sternwheeler. Enjoy all you can eat Southern style buffet highlighted by music featuring the Nashville sounds. $12.50 per person.

Dinner cruise aboard the Belle Carol

Pie Wagons

BROWN'S DINER / 2106 Blair Blvd. / Open 10:30 a.m. til midnight 7 days a week / 269-5509

Thought Pie Wagons went out with Okies, Gary Cooper and James Cagney movies and "Brother Can You Spare Me A Dime?" This is really a funky little beer joint that serves a great hamburger. It also proves that dimensions are unimportant when it comes to a good cold beer.

EDMUND'S RESTAURANT / 118 12th Avenue South / Breakfast and Lunch 5:30-2:30 Mon.-Fri., Sat. 6-10 a.m. / 256-5893

This place may not qualify as a genuine pie wagon but it's too good to leave out. Besides, it is so far off the road and so innocuous it might pass for one. Lots of good country cooking.

In the Countryside

Franklin

MISS DAISEY'S TEA ROOM / Carter's Court / Lunch 11-2 p.m. Mon.-Sat. with Sunday buffet 11-2 p.m. / 790-1934

A favorite lunch time place for visitors. A special part of this charming little shopping area. Very good food and a pleasant, light feeling to this popular spot.

Ashland City

Bill's and Brantley's are two favorite catfish eateries in Cheatham County. Pour yourself a drink or two and then strike out. No alcoholic beverages served. Call for directions. These places close early so check before you go. Then enjoy the food and the drive which is beautiful in spots. Bill's Restaurant (792-9193) and Brantley's Restaurant (792-4703).

Clarksville

HACHLAND HALL / 647-4084

You'll need reservations but this place is widely known for their truly good food. Delicacies, meats, vegetables and desserts all cooked and served with a flair. Haute cuisine a la Tennessee. Phila was in charge of food preparation when the United Nations delegates visited Nashville in 1976. It was delicious!

Brentwood

SQUIRE'S TABLE / Franklin Road at Old Hickory Blvd. / Dinner only / 373-0660

Tally ho! The cozy warmth of this rustic restaurant beckon images of hounds and horses and fox hunts. Good steaks and attentive service. Nice for a change of pace.

NOBLE / Franklin Road at Old Hickory Blvd. / Mon.-Sun. 6:30-8:30 p.m. / 373-1166

Country cooking and an easy atmosphere. Like eating in your kitchen. Only better! Good vegetables and meats.

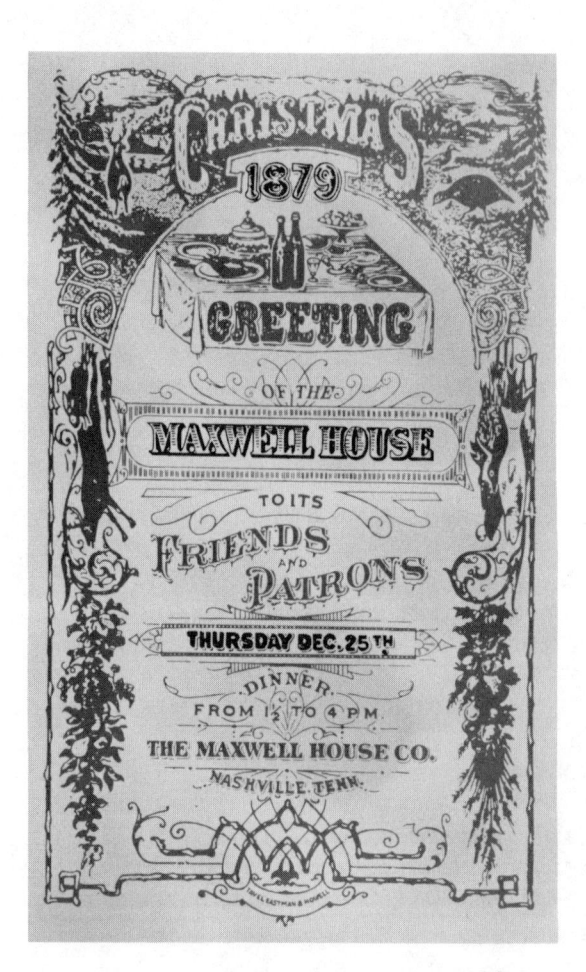

Cafeterias and Buffets

HERMITAGE HOUSE SMORGASBORD / 4144 Lebanon Road / Lunch
   11-2:30 p.m. Dinner 4:30-8:30 p.m., Sunday 11-8:30 p.m. / Very good
   and near Opryland / 833-9525

SILVER WINGS RESTAURANT / 1 International Plaza / Lunch 11:30-3 p.m.
   Dinner 5-11 p.m. / Great buffet / 361-7220

MELROSE HOUSE SMORGASBORD / 2600 Bransford House / Lunch
   11-2 p.m., Dinner 5-8:30 p.m. til 9:30 p.m. Fri. & Sat. / 255-3193

SPEEDY'S GRILL / 401 Monroe Street / Lunch and dinner 5 a.m. til 5 p.m.
   Mon.-Fri. / 255-6693

MORRISON'S CAFETERIA / 7 locations

Chains and Fast Food

Ireland's (Nashville's own. Try their steak and biscuits. Delicious.)
Jolly Ox (Steak and Ale in other parts of the country)
Shoney's
Pizza Hut
Hungry Fisherman
Red Lobster
Bonanza Steaks
Captain D's Seafood
Jerry's
Judy's
Wendy's
McDonald's
El Chico
Krystal
Kentucky Fried Chicken
Arby's
Long John Silver's

Listings: Where to Find . . .

Sunday Brunch

T.G.I. FRIDAY'S / 2214 Elliston Place / Menu includes champagne, eggs benedict
   and more / Reservations suggested / 329-9575

HYATT REGENCY / 623 Union Street / Sumptuous buffet of delectables from scotch eggs to salmon / 259-1234

OPRYLAND HOTEL / 2800 Opryland Drive / A touch of New Orleans around the fountain / 889-1000

GOLD RUSH / 2205 Elliston Place / 327-2809

LAUGHING MAN / 1926 Division / Vegetarian / 320-9071

ELLISTON HALL / 217 Louise Avenue / 327-0302

MAUDE'S COURTYARD / 1911 Broadway / 320-0543

BISHOP'S CORNER / 3201 West End / 383-9288

SHENANIGAN'S / 3324 West End / 298-4470

O'CHARLEY'S / 402 21st Avenue South / 327-3773

Others Open Sunday

Dynasty (lunch and dinner)
Peddler (dinner only)
Fifth Quarter (dinner)
The Shack (lunch and dinner)
Sperry's (dinner)
Smuggler's (dinner)
Houston's (lunch and dinner)
Kobe Steaks (dinner)
Villa Romano (dinner)
Carmen's (lunch and dinner)
Viscaya (dinner)
Blue Hawaii (lunch and dinner)
Maharajah (dinner)
Loveless Motel Restaurant (breakfast, lunch and dinner)
Captain Ray's Sailmaker (dinner)
Maple Fox (dinner)
Miss Daisey's Tea Room (lunch and dinner)
Noble's Restaurant (lunch and dinner)
Belle Meade Motel Restaurant (breakfast, lunch and dinner)
Hermitage House Smorgasbord (lunch and dinner)
Silver Wings Restaurant (lunch and dinner)
Morrison's Cafeteria (lunch and dinner)

Stars' Kitchens

GEORGE JONES' POSSUM HOLLER / Printer's Alley at Commerce / Country cooking: beans, ham hock and corn bread as well as country ham and steak and biscuits / 254-1431

BOOTS RANDOLPH'S / Printer's Alley / Dinner: steaks and king crab / 256-5500

All-Niters

MALONE'S / 407 1st Avenue South / country ham, biscuits and gravies / a special place!
CHARLIE NICKENS / 305 Jefferson Street / barbeque since 1934 — eat in or carry out.
KEY TRUCK STOP / 100 West Trinity Lane
SAMBO'S / 2304 Brick Church Pike
KRYSTAL / 13 locations
WAFFLE HOUSE / 7 locations
JERRY'S / 4 locations
HUDDLE HOUSE / 231 7th Avenue North
DENNY'S / Plus Park Blvd.
DOWNTOWNER MOTOR INN RESTAURANT / 622 Two Mile Pike in Goodlettsville

Good or Great Breakfasts

LOVELESS MOTEL RESTAURANT / Highway 100 South / Great country ham and biscuits / 327-3773

BELLE MEADE MOTEL RESTAURANT / 5133 Harding Road / Terrific breakfast steak / 352-2317

MORRIS ZAGER / 221 6th Avenue / 255-3108

INTERNATIONAL HOUSE OF PANCAKES / 2020 Broadway / 320-0562

HOLIDAY INN VANDERBILT / 2613 West End / Varied buffet / 383-1147

MALONE'S / 407 1st Avenue South / 251-9589

KRYSTAL / 13 locations

Specialties

Hamburgers

FRIDAY'S / 2214 Elliston Place / 329-9575

WENDY'S / 8 locations

McDONALDS / 15 locations

KRYSTAL / 13 locations

ROTIER'S / 2413 Elliston / 327-9872

O'CHARLEY'S / 402 21st Avenue South / 327-3773

Chili

MISSISSIPPI WHISKERS / 1713 Church / 320-9118

FRIDAY'S / 2214 Elliston Place / 329-9575

VARALLO'S / 817 Church Street / 256-9106

MARCHETTI'S / 102 19th Street / 322-9729

BBQ

BAR-B-CUTIE / 432 Murfreesboro Road / 256-9484

CENTERPOINT / 1212 W. Main Street / Hendersonville / 824-9330

MARY'S / 1108 Jefferson Street / 256-7696

CHARLIE NICKENS / 305 Jefferson Street / 251-9158

WHITE COTTAGE / 1102 3rd Avenue North / 251-9120

BOB EARL'S MARKET / 1500 Robinson Road / Old Hickory / 847-4566
   (Our favorite! Don't let the address fool you. It's just straight out Old Hickory Blvd. in Old Hickory across from the Food Town. Mostly carry out although they do have a couple of dinette tables in the next room. Grab a couple of beers and head for the lake!!)

Desserts & Sweets

SATSUMA / 417 Union Street / all kinds including freshly made ice creams / 256-5211

```
SATURDAY - 1978                    ELLISTON PLACE SODA SHOP
                    PLATE LUNCHES:
ROAST ROUND OF BEEF - BROWN GRAVY . . . . . . . . $2.10
BAKED SUGAR-CURED HAM . . . . . . . . . . . . . . $2.10
SOUTHERN FRIED CHICKEN . . . . . . . . . . . . . . $2.10
                 CHOICE OF THREE VEGETABLES:
   STEWED TURNIPS    SLICED TOMATO    WHIPPED POTATOES
   GREEN BEANS       COTTAGE CHEESE   MIXED VEGETABLES
   BAKED SQUASH      CONGEALED FRUIT SALAD   COLE SLAW
***************************************************
$1.80                 VEGETABLE PLATE              $1.80
CHOICE OF FOUR VEGETABLES (Listed above) WITH HOT BREAD
***************************************************
$3.25          FRIED SHRIMP or OYSTER DINNER       $3.25
HALF-DOZEN PREMIUM LARGE SHRIMP or EXTRA SELECT OYSTERS
               FRENCH FRIES & COLE SLAW
***************************************************
$1.95            SPECIAL FISH DINNER               $1.95
      FRIED FILET OF COD, FRENCH FRIES & COLE SLAW
***************************************************
$2.75            CHICKEN PLATE SPECIAL             $2.75
   3 PIECES CHICKEN, TOSSED GREEN SALAD, FRENCH FRIES
                  CHOICE OF DRESSING
***************************************************
$2.75                  FRUIT PLATE                 $2.75
      ASSORTED FRUITS, COTTAGE CHEESE or ORANGE SHERBET
                   RAISIN BREAD TOAST
***************************************************
90¢              HOLLYWOOD SALAD BOWL              90¢
      FRUIT, COTTAGE CHEESE, CELERY & CARROT STICKS
***************************************************
$2.50                  COLD PLATE                  $2.50
     BAKED HAM, POTATO SALAD, DEVILED EGG, SLICED TOMATO,
          FRUIT, SLICED CHEESE, PICKLE GARNISH
                  SERVED WITH RYE BREAD
***************************************************
                       STEAK PLATES
T-BONE STEAK . . . . . . . . . . . . . . . . . . . $3.50
CHOICE SIRLOIN STRIP . . . . . . . . . . . . . . . $4.00
WESTERN CLUB STEAK . . . . . . . . . . . . . . . . $3.25
   ABOVE SERVED WITH FRENCH FRIES & TOSSED GREEN SALAD
***************************************************
HOT ROAST BEEF SANDWICH, POTATOES & SLAW . . . . . $1.90
STEAKBURGER, FRENCH FRIES & COLE SLAW . . . . . . . $1.75
```

ELLISTON PLACE SODA SHOP / 2111 Elliston Place / 327-1090

CANDYLAND / 631 Church / 256-5946 / 2916 West End / 383-4164

YOGURT BARN / 413 Union Street / 242-9468

KRISPY KREME DOUGHNUTS / four locations / call and find out when they pull them from the oven. Usually around 8 p.m. every evening. Melt in your mouth . . .

DAYLIGHT DOUGHNUT SHOP / 2502 Franklin Road / 292-8594

DOUGHNUT DEN / 4002 Granny White Pike / 297-0345

BASKIN ROBBINS / 10 locations

BISHOP'S CORNER / 3201 West End Avenue / (fudge pie) / 383-9288

SHONEY'S / 37 locations in Middle Tennessee / (strawberry pie and hot fudge cake)

GERST HOUSE / 228 Woodland Street / (apple strudel) / 256-9760

CIRACO'S ITALIAN RESTAURANT / 212 21st Avenue South / (pastries) / 327-9726

HOUSTON'S / 3000 West End Avenue / (bananas foster) / 269-3481

Bakeries

BECKER'S / 2600 12th Avenue South / 383-5554

SUNFLOWER / 6002 Highway 100 / 356-8546

Restaurants by Location

DOWNTOWN (Lunch)

>Langford's
>Candyland
>Zager's

Satsuma
Hyatt Regency
Varallo's
McDonald's
Shoney's
Cain Sloan Iris Room
Harvey's Basement Dinette Fountain

HERMITAGE/OPRYLAND (Lunch)

Hermitage House
Pizza Hut
McDonald's
Bob Earl's BBQ – Old Hickory

MUSIC ROW/VANDERBILT

Ireland's
O'Charley's
Ciraco's
Arby's
The Peddler
Kentucky Fried Chicken
Hap Townes
Laughing Man
Maude's Courtyard
Spats
Wendy's

How to Pick a Restaurant*

Invariably most men will answer: ask a cab driver, bellman, or desk clerk. Maybe, but we've always ended up with indigestion following that approach in a strange city.

Our suggestion: buy a guide (like *The Good Times Guide To Nashville*) or pick up one of the free dining or entertainment guides or glance through the entertainment section of the local newspaper. If any restaurant feature a Holiday Awards designation, choose that one. Ditto Mobil or any other recognizable rating. Most restaurants are proud of the distinction and emphasize it in their advertisements.

If none of the restaurants in the city rate a special designation, then deciding where to dine becomes more of a challenge. A hotel dining room is almost always safe, if not exciting.

Restaurants located near universities or exclusive shopping areas seem to attract a more sophisticated and demanding clientele and a full parking lot can be a good sign. (Unless the locales have no taste or the establishment is widely known for its family prices. Then it is round 'em up and herd 'em out.) Finally, consider asking a pretty woman for the best place to dine. Chances are she has been there!

Deadline Additions

L'AUBERGE / 2121 West End / Dinner: Mon.-Fri. 6:30 - 10 p.m., Sat. til 11 p.m. / 320-0088

Very good food and excellent service. Haute cuisine. Dover sole and the rack of lamb are fresh and very good. Very nice wine list. Good desserts. And Bertrand, the maitre d', charms you with his French (Brittany) accent.

ANDERSON'S CAJUN'S WHARF / 901 Cowan Street / Hours: Dinner 5 p.m. til 11 p.m. Mon.-Thurs., til midnight Fri. & Sat. Lounge 4:30 til 2 p.m. Mon.-Sat. / 254-7711

Cajun creole fare. Motif . . . great! Fish nets, cypress siding, and artwork of dark-haired Cajuns, swamps and shrimp boats. Fresh oysters, lobsters, shrimp, and crawfish. A great Sazerac Bar with live entertainment. Food generally spicy and lots of it . . . family style. A very popular place down in the warehouse district overlooking the Cumberland River.

FANTIQUE'S / 2609 West End across from Centennial Park / Brunch and lunch daily 11-5 p.m., Dinner daily 5-11 p.m., Sunday jazz brunch New Orleans style & late supper 11 p.m. til 2:30 a.m. Piano bar 5-9 p.m. and Happy Hour 4-7 p.m. Live entertainment 9:30-2 a.m. Mon.-Sat. / 292-5515

Take an old A & P food store and gut it. Fill it with ornate furniture and furnishings. One room . . . all wicker. The next Victorian. The third a cozy library and the fourth a country front porch. The food is not nearly so interesting as the decor! But it is a very popular place and the prices are reasonable. The piano music, the Sunday jazz brunch and the Jimmy McGowan trio are great drawing cards.

NIGHTCLUBS
LISTENING ROOMS
BEER TAVERNS

Nightclubs

Printer's Alley

      BLACK POODLE / 256-9552
      Exotic dancers.

      BOOTS RANDOLPH / 256-5500
      Appearing nightly Mr. Sax himself. Dining: steaks and king crab.

      CAPTAIN'S TABLE / 256-3353
      A popular night spot. Good Food. Steaks and Lobster.

      SKULL'S RAINBOW / 251-9076
      Exotic dancers and comedy routines nightly.

      CAROUSEL / 244-8391
      Home of country music entertainer Ronnie Prophet. Las Vegas style entertainment. Specialty: steak and ribs.

      EMBERS WESTERN ROOM / 256-9339
      Johnny Paycheck among others often performs here. Check it out.

White Rabbit Saloon in Lynchburg at the turn of the century

Others:

    BLUE MAX / 259-1234 / Entertainment nightly / located in the Hyatt Regency.

    GEORGE JONES POSSUM HOLLER / 254-1431 / Commerce & Printer's Alley / Live music. Country snackings and your favorite drink.

THE NASHVILLE PALACE / 885-1540 / Music Valley Drive
near Opryland / A 600-seat supper club serving steaks and lobster. A swinging night spot.

STARLITE / 865-9709 / 3976 Dickerson Road / Entertainment nightly. Dining and dancing. Steaks and your favorite cocktail. Dance contest every Thursday.

FOUR GUYS HARMONY HOUSE / 256-0188 / 407 Murfreesboro Road / Live entertainment. A very popular place.

STAGE DOOR LOUNGE / 889-1000 / Opryland Hotel / Las Vegas style entertainment. Two shows nightly.

Disco

SMUGGLER'S / 361-4440 / 1204 Murfreesboro Road

Exotic Dancers

CLASSIC CAT II / 6th and Broad / 242-9183

BLACK POODLE / Printer's Alley / 256-9552

SKULL'S RAINBOW / Printer's Alley / 251-9076

Listening Rooms

EXIT IN / 2208 Elliston Place / 327-2784
Performances by entertainers like Waylon Jennings, Doc Watson, Earl Scruggs and many, many others over the years, and a following by folks who want to hear good music have created this first-rate, mellow listening room. Well-known from L.A. to N.Y. Check out and see who is playing. Then go. Attend a writer's night and hear the artists perform the songs they have written.

OLD TIME PICKING PARLOR / 105 2nd Avenue North / 256-5720
This really nitty-gritty little place in the old warehouse district downtown is another favorite. Not as sophisticated as the Exit In, but it is low-key and easy.

BLUE GRASS INN / 1914 Broadway / 320-0624
Hear traditional bluegrass here. A favorite of college students.

Exit/In

DUSTY ROAD TAVERN / 114 Woodland / 251-9904
   Continuous entertainment daily from 1 p.m. 'til 3 a.m. Country and bluegrass.

Beer Taverns for Good Ole Boys

TOOTSIE'S ORCHID LOUNGE / 422 Broadway / 251-9725

BROWN'S DINER / 2106 Blair Blvd. / 269-5509

WAXIE'S / 2414 Elliston Place / 327-9752

PAGE'S DINER / 1102 Gallatin Road / 226-9322

VILLAGER TAVERN / 1719 21st Avenue South / 292-9142

JOE'S VILLAGE INN / 4107 Hillsboro Road / 297-9115

Bars and Lounges Open Past Midnight

Ever feel like bar hopping during the week and can't find a bar open? Ever wanted a night cap after a late dinner and all the lounges are locking up? Feel like a night owl and there's no place to go? Try the following. They specialize in staying open late!

CAPTAIN'S TABLE / 333½ Church Street	'til 3 am
BLACK POODLE / Printer's Alley	'til 3 am
GEORGE JONES POSSUM HOLLER / Commerce & Printer's Alley	'til 3 am
FOUR GUYS HARMONY HOUSE / 407 Murfreesboro Road	'til 3 am
T.G.I. FRIDAY'S / 2214 Elliston Place	'til 2 am
GOLD RUSH / 2205 Elliston Place	'til 2 am
JUDY WEST'S PLACE / 31 White Bridge Road	'til 2 am
OPRYLAND HOTEL / Stage Door	'til 2 am
Saloon	'til 2 am
Veranda	'til 2:30
SKULL'S RAINBOW / Printer's Alley	'til 3 am
STARLITE / 3976 Dickerson Road	'til 3 am
CAROUSEL / Printer's Alley	'til 3 am
EMBERS WESTERN ROOM / Printer's Alley	'til 3 am
BLUE MAX / Hyatt Regency	'til 2 am

Note: Most bars and lounges are open later on weekends ... Sperry's, Jolly Ox, Ireland's, Shenanigan's, and others.

Happy Hour/Cocktails

HOUSTON'S / 3000 West End Avenue / 269-3481

SHENANIGAN'S / 3324 West End Avenue / 298-4479

FRIDAY'S / 2214 Elliston Place / 329-9575

HYATT REGENCY / 623 Union Street / 259-1234

FIFTH QUARTER / 295 E. Thompson Lane / 242-3583

JOLLY OX / 4 locations

Other Night Clubs

COTTON PLANTATION / 1366 Murfreesboro Road
HERR HARRY'S PHRANKS AND STEINS / 1909 West End Avenue
LEO'S DISCO / 1719 West End
MET / 240 Cumberland Bend in MetroCenter
RHINESTONE COWBOY / 102 3rd Avenue North
RINKY DINKS / 4104 Hillsboro Road
WOODEN HORSE / Hillsboro Village
WIND IN THE WILLOWS / 2205 State Street near Elliston Place
ROLLER COASTER / Nolensville Road and Haywood Lane behind Tusculum Center
SPRING WATER / 27th Avenue North near West End
ROCK HARBOUR / 6590 Robertson Road

SOUVENIRS

Trinkets and Special Reminders of Your Visit to Music City U.S.A.

The following stores are the most popular souvenir shops offering a wide and varied selection of standard items. Of course, there are miscellaneous items available in other gift shops located within major attractions, such as the Hermitage and the Parthenon, and limited lines are also to be found in hotels. But for *special* reminders see the next page!

REBEL TRADING POST / 431 Broad near the Ryman Auditorium

COUNTRY CORNER / 117 16th Ave. S.

COUNTRY MUSIC HALL OF FAME / 4 Music Square E.

MUSIC ROW COUNTRY STORE / 1530 Demonbreun

OPRYLAND U.S.A. / Opryland Drive

CRACKER BARREL OLD COUNTRY STORES / (several locations along the interstate)

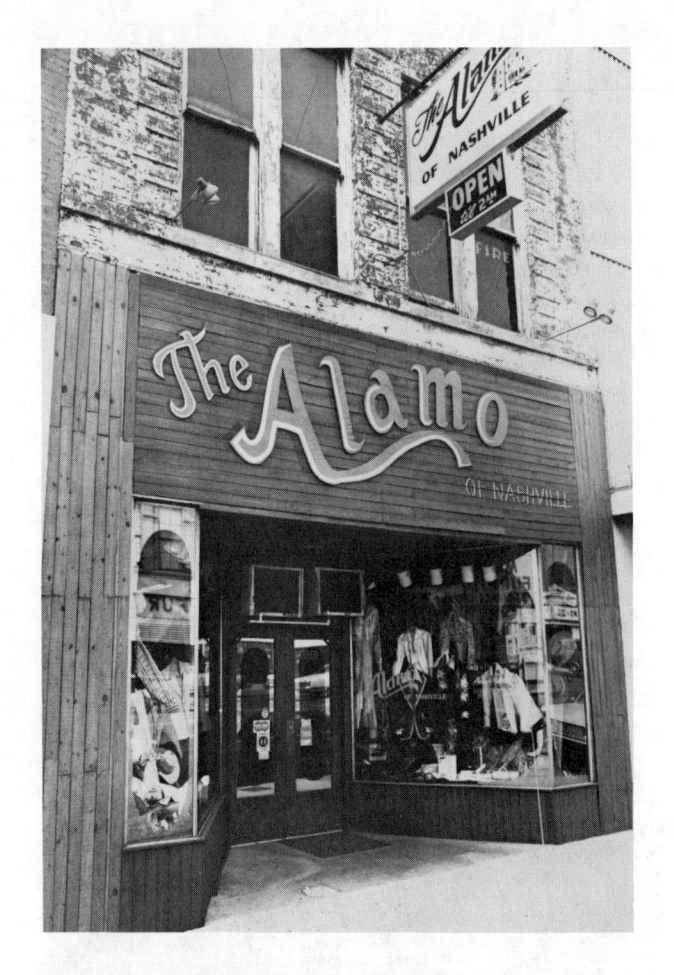

Special Reminders *(and where to buy them):*

Western wear — shirts, pants, jeans. Where: The Alamo, Loretta Lynn's and Sundance.

Records — country. Where: Ernest Tubb Record Shop and Sue Kline Music Shop. (Full line record shops: Music Mart USA and Discount Records)

Musical instruments — guitars, fiddles, banjos and dulcimers. Where: Sho-Bud Guitars, Old Time Picking Parlor, Gruhn Guitars, Tut Taylor (dulcimers handmade) and the pawn shops along Lower Broad. (Gallagher Guitar Shop in Wartrace, Tennessee, south of Nashville about 75 miles, has also produced guitars for such folk as Randy Scruggs, Doc Watson, Neil Diamond, and Peter, Paul and Mary.)

Stormy Ryman

Imagine the silent, majestic old Ryman Auditorium captured on poster during a storm. Lightening crackling overhead. Mysterious, sad . . . vulnerable.

Country music fans who enjoy nostalgia and photography will like the stormy poster of the Ryman available at Goodies Warehouse on Second Ave. N. for $15. Photographed by Jim McGuire of Grease Brothers photography.

Tennessee hams, molasses, cracklings, spices, teas and gourds — edible and attractive reminders. Where: Farmer's Market downtown or local grocery stores. Loveless Restaurant and the Cracker Barrel Country Stores also sell Tennessee hams. Tip: Use the gourds for water dippers, wall hangings or plant containers. A grouping in a basket on the table looks nice, too. If you see any sassafrass, buy some. Boil it in water and it makes the most delicious and fragrant tea. Also look around for some cracklings, the fried pork skins are great in cornbread.

Crafts — quilts, baskets and more. Where: Goodies, Craft Cranny, the Artisan House, Carter's Court, the Cracker Barrel, the Tennessee Crafts Fair in May and from individual craftsmen. (Call the Tennessee Artist and Craftsmen Association, 242-2518, or drop by the crafts division of the Tennessee Arts Commission in the Capitol Hill Building across the street from the Hyatt Regency for further information.)

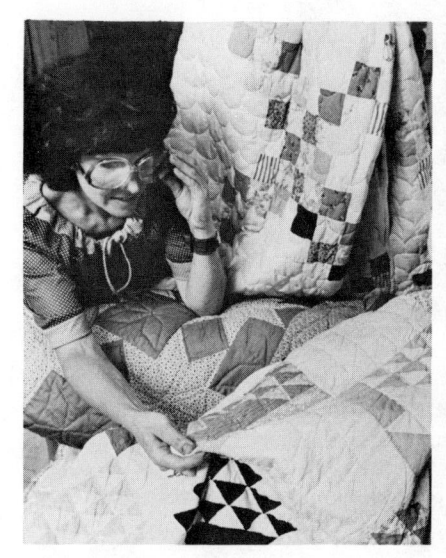

Goodies

Antiques — pie safes, crocks, old ice boxes and more. Where: local antique shops, antique malls and the Nashville Flea Market the last weekend of every month.

Stained glass — specially made. Where: Emmanuel Stained Glass Studio, next door to Maranatha Crafts, another intriguing shop on 16th Ave. S.

Art — Tennessee scenes by wild life naturalists. Where: Raintree Gallery in Franklin and Greystone Gallery in Nashville.

Sundance

Jack Daniel's souvenirs — tins, shot glasses and more. Where: Cain Sloan department stores and the Lynchburg Hardware Store in Lynchburg.

Goo Goo — candy bars. Where: any grocery store or drive-in market. Buy a dozen for family and friends!

Christmas Specials

Spice round and plum pudding are two traditional specials for Nashvillians. Spice round, beef injected with plugs of spicy marbling, is available only in Nashville grocery stores during the season and is prepared by Baltz Brothers Packing. Meanwhile, Warrenton Old English Plum Pudding Ltd. sells marvelous tins of delicious pudding, ready to be steamed, and tosses in a great recipe for a topping sauce. Christmas is special and so are these dishes.

For the Connoisseur

Gourmet tidbits, aphrodisiacs, amulets and miscellany

Where to find . . .

Oysters on the half shell /fresh and baked
    New Orleans Manor and Seafood Feast Restaurant
    Julian's Restaurant
    The Shack Restaurant
    Brass Rail Restaurant
    Sunflower Grocery (fish market)

Frog legs
    New Orleans Manor and Seafood Feast Restaurant
    Little Fish and Oyster Co. (fish market)

Escargot
    Sperry's Restaurant
    L'Auberge Restaurant

Hearts of palm
    Julian's Restaurant
    Brass Rail Restaurant

Perrier water and caviar
    Julian's Restaurant
    L'Auberge Restaurant
    Green Hills Market (lots of special brands, produce, meats and seafood in this well-stocked and elite grocery store)

Quiche
    Houston's Restaurant

Cheesecake
    Friday's Restaurant
    Fifth Quarter Restaurant
    Morris Zager Delicatessen
    Martin Lipke (grocer's section)

Expresso and other after dinner coffees
    Julian's Restaurant
    Villa Romano Restaurant
    (Cookware and Cutlery Shop on 21st Ave. S. also has a variety of imported coffee beans)

Restaurants with good wine lists
    Julian's
    Brass Rail
    Sperry's

Wine and liquor stores (the best stocked)
    Demetros Liquor Store and Wine Mart
    Green Hills Liquors

Health food stores/restaurants
    Sunshine Grocery
    The Grateful Breadbox
    The Laughing Man Restaurant

Famous Amos Cookies
    N.Y. N.Y. Boutique, Bavarian Village

Baubles (gems, jewelry and more*)*
Old and unusual (also designer) shops:
    Richter's
    Bem's
    Anthony's
    Sain, Wolk, Stieff-Jaccard and Broadnax also carries interesting pieces of new and quality jewelry.

Orchids, tulips, gardenias and roses
    Arts and Petals (orchids)
    Tulip Tree (all manner of fresh cut flowers in season)
    Tom Harrison (romantic little bouquets)
    Geddes Douglas Nursery (gardenias and hot house varieties)

Silks and designer fabrics
    Village Fabric Shop

Gilbert's Liquor Store

"Beg your pardon."
"Excuse me."
"It is right behind you."
Gilbert's Liquor Store, Nashville's oldest in its original location on Charlotte Avenue could be called quaint, cozy or cramped, depending upon your reaction to claustrophobia. But in this day of super flash and suburban sprawl, it is nice to be nose to nose with a Rothchild wine or Polish vodka.

    Gilbert's draws a varied clientele from the tweedy set of nearby colleges to the poorer, soul brothers who buy Ripple wine in large quantities. Mr. Isadore Gilbert, the proprietor, will order special brands for you and the establishment carries a surprisingly wide selection despite its limited space!

MORE TO DO: THEATRE, SYMPHONY, CINEMA, MUSEUMS AND ART GALLERIES

Theater and Symphony

ADVENT THEATRE / 1200 17th Avenue South / 327-0373
> Professional theatre is center stage here. Productions run the gamut from comedies like "Luv" to dramas such as "Hedda Gabler." The theater itself is a renovated church and rectory where playwright Tennessee Williams once stayed while visiting relatives. This theater company hopes eventually to be at home in the new Tennessee Performing Arts Center scheduled to open in autumn of 1979.

CHILDREN'S THEATRE / 724 2nd Avenue South / 254-9103
> Since 1930 this theater has been creating live performances for hundreds of thousands of young people. Today it is the oldest, largest and most successful organization of its kind in the U.S. It was the first children's theater to perform at the Eisenhower Theatre of the Kennedy Center in Washington, D.C. And the company has toured Europe. Adults will enjoy their productions, too.

ENSEMBLE THEATRE / 809 16th Avenue South / 329-1689

> Off-beat and witty, this theatre company has earned a good reputation and local following. It is "theater-in-residence" at Scarritt College.

Nashville Symphony

Others:

BARN DINNER THEATER / 8204 Highway 100 / 646-3111

CIRCLE THEATRE / 4102 Hillsboro Road / 256-6855

THEATRE NASHVILLE / 218 3rd Avenue North / 383-3473

NASHVILLE SYMPHONY / 1805 West End Avenue / Performances: War Memorial Auditorium / 329-3033

Since 1920 this symphony has been around providing Nashville with its own particular sound. Blair Academy and Peabody College along with area businesses have contributed heavily to this community organization, both in terms of talent, time and interest. Not to mention sustaining gifts and memberships. The gala Symphony Outing every fall at Opryland features a big name headliner for entertainment and it is a popular social event as is the annual Italian Street Fair.

Cinema

Check the individual theaters for offerings, times and locations. Also during the school year Vanderbilt's Sarratt Cinema Center shows foreign, classic, documentary and short subject films in cooperation with the Nashville Film Society. And in early June, Vanderbilt is home for the enormously popular Sinking Creek Film Celebration. Check for dates and features.

Museums

CUMBERLAND SCIENCE / 800 Ridley / Open 10 - 5 p.m. Tues. - Sat 1 - 5 p.m. Sun. Closed Mon. / Admission: Adults $1 Children (5 - 17) 50 cents, under 5 free / 242-1858

16,000 artifacts from fossils to foxes and dolls to deers are housed in this museum. There are life-like sculptures of wildflowers, a planetarium, Indian artifacts, dioramas and a live animal room.

"Hedda Gabler" at the Advent Theatre

Others previously mentioned under attractions:

    PARTHENON / Centennial Park / Indian artifacts / 383-6411

    TENNESSEE STATE MUSEUM / War Memorial Building / 741-2692

    FT. NASHBOROUGH / First Ave. near Lower Broad / 255-8192

    HERMITAGE / Rachel's Lane / Hermitage / 889-2941

    COUNTRY MUSIC HALL OF FAME AND MUSEUM / 4 Music Square East / 244-2522

    COUNTRY MUSIC WAX MUSEUM / 118 16th Ave. S. / 256-2490

    OPRYLAND U.S.A. / Opryland Drive / 889-6611

    TENNESSEE BOTANICAL GARDENS AND FINE ARTS CENTER / Cheekwood at Cheek Road / 352-5310

    HANK WILLIAMS MUSEUM / 115 16th Ave. S. / 254-7548

Art Galleries

PEABODY COLLEGE COHEN MEMORIAL ART GALLERY / 21st Ave. S. / 327-8178

FISK UNIVERSITY'S VAN VECHTEN GALLERY AND LIBRARY / 17th Ave. N. / 329-9111

VANDERBILT OLD GYM ART GALLERY / West End Avenue / 322-2831

UNIVERSITY CLUB / 2402 Garland Ave. / 327-4371

PARTHENON GALLERY / Centennial Park / 383-6411

Emperor Jones by Aaron Douglas at the Fisk University gallery

Others:

AL'S CUSTOM FRAMES AND ART GALLERY / 2605 Westwood Drive / wild life, sporting and western originals / 297-0618

ANTIQUARIAN GALLERY / 4034 Hillsboro Road / antique prints and paintings / 298-1225

COLLECTOR'S GALLERY / 2401 Abbott Martin Road / American impressionism and contemporary paintings and graphics / 383-3120

DILLINGHAM GALLERY / 2213 Bandywood / 385-3120

RAINTREE GALLERY / Carter's Court / limited edition prints, paintings and gift items / 790-1764

LYZON / 411 Thompson Lane / framing and an interesting selection of various types of paintings and prints / 256-7538

GRAYSTONE PRESS AND GALLERY / 207 Louise Ave. / beautiful wildlife and pastoral Tennessee scenes and contemporary designs, too / 327-9497

"Really Rosie" at the Academy (Children's) Theatre

Note: Check the Sunday Tennessean for complete details, general descriptions, hours and special shows. Admission to all of the above is free.

Wyeth to Warhol and Coming: Stieglitz

Cheekwood (Tennessee Botanical Gardens and Fine Arts Center) offers an array of visual delights. The art gallery includes orientals, watercolors, English portraits, modern and contemporary and special collections usually. The permanent exhibits includes pieces by Red Grooms, Larry Rivers, Jamie Wyeth and Andy Warhol. Admission: Adults $2.

Meanwhile, the Fisk University Van Vechten Gallery is scheduled to be the home of the Alfred Stieglitz collection which includes works by Cezanne, Picasso, Renoir and others. The collection, donated to the university by the artist's wife, Georgia O'Keefe, years ago, is being refurbished in New York and will be on permanent display at the gallery once restoration is completed. Til then, there is a fine exhibit of African art for viewing. Admission: free.

Gardens and Parks

TENNESSEE BOTANICAL GARDENS AND FINE ARTS CENTER
    AT CHEEKWOOD / Cheek Road

Wild flowers, trees and shrubs in the spring, summer water lilies in the grotto, camellias and tulips in the garden, greenhouse orchids, herb, perennial and Japanese sand gardens, autumn foliage, holly and the trees of Christmas make Cheekwood a year 'round experience. Go. Tour the mansion, view the art collection and enjoy lunch there, too.

CENTENNIAL PARK / West End Avenue

Visit the Japanese Garden in the spring and summer. It is gorgeous then. Also tour the Parthenon and walk around Watauga Lake.

PERCY AND EDWIN WARNER PARK / Old Hickory Blvd. off Highway 100 S.

Lose yourself in this sprawling park system. It is Nashville's largest — 2,700 acres. Riding stables, trails, covered picnic sites, baseball diamonds and more. The Iroquois Steeplechase is held there annually. There is also a model plane field and Harpeth Hills golf course is nearby.

Cheekwood

SHELBY PARK / East Nashville

> Much more tame than its west Nashville counterparts. Nice lake, covered picnic sites, lots of local league baseball action here, tennis courts and for a family gathering reserve Sycamore Lodge. Children's playground nearby.

RADNOR LAKE / Off Hillsboro Road past Green Hills

> Often forgotten, but this fragile natural area, 80 acres of water, is a great place for bird watchers, geologists and wildlife lovers. 3½ miles of trails, 50 species of wild flowers and 222 species of birds have been identified there. Like a fine lady, there is a "look, but don't touch" philosophy here . . . no fishing, no picking the flowers.

Three Great Ideas for a Picnic Lunch

Ask the Satsuma Tea Room to fix up a couple of box lunches. They are terrific. Or simply pick up a box or bucket of Col. Sanders' Kentucky Fried Chicken. And don't forget . . . baloney, crackers and cheese taste good too.

Cheekwood

Summa Cum Laude — What's Worth Seeing on Nashville's Campuses

PEABODY COLLEGE

>The most aesthetic. Landscaped quad with classical revival buildings. The domed Social Religious Building crowns the view. This well-known teacher's college boasts the Kennedy Center on Education and Human Research. Visit the Cohen Art Gallery and view the beautiful mosaic by Ben Shahn in the Human Development Laboratory building.

VANDERBILT UNIVERSITY

>Sprawling. Nashville's most prestigious. Victorian and oxford gothic buildings plus modern ones, brick sidewalks and lots of trees make up this campus. The school was a gift from Cornelius Vanderbilt and is often called the "Harvard of the South." It has been the spawning ground for the Fugitive literary movement and its spokesmen played a role in the South's Agrarian movement years ago. Interested in foreign films or the classics? Check with Sarratt Cinema during the school year for dates and times of the Nashville Film Society series. Also visit the Old Gym art gallery and there are manuscripts of William Faulkner in the Joint University Library. Impact Symposium and the annual spring jazz concert are other highlights.

SCARRITT

Near the Upper Room. Charming vari-colored cloisters and chapels. This Methodist college trains missionaries for world-wide ministries.

FISK UNIVERSITY

The entire campus has recently been declared a National Historic Landmark. This major black college is famed for its "Jubilee Singers" who toured Europe in 1871 to help raise money to build the six-story Victorian gothic Jubilee Hall which is still standing. Visit the Memorial Chapel where Martin Luther King often spoke before he rose to national prominence. And check out the Van Vechten Gallery which houses contemporary art and there is an outstanding African art collection on the third floor of the library.

BELMONT

Once one of the finest homes in the South, the Italian Renaissance villa is the main administration building. Rather dog-eared now, the campus was formerly the old Ward-Belmont Finishing School. Alumni: Minnie Pearl and Clare Boothe Luce. Wish someone would restore it to its former self a´ la´ gardens, flower beds and fountains. The gazebo still stands.

MEHARRY

There are several contemporary and strikingly modern buildings on this campus. It is an international training ground for black doctors and dentists.

TENNESSEE STATE UNIVERSITY

Driving by this rambling brick and mortar school you would never suspect that it has produced some of the best athletes in the world. Its Tigerbelle track team is internationally renowned. Alumni: Wilma Rudolph, among others.

OTHERS

There are many other schools, colleges and universities in Nashville. Explore them for yourself. Some are often overlooked, like the Free Will Baptist College campus which takes in some of the finer old homes along West End.

THINGS TO DO FOR FREE
(and 4-almost-free)

* Explore the Cumberland Science Museum. Tuesdays are free. (16,000 artifacts from fossils to foxes and dolls to deer. A live animal room, too!)

*Ride the Clees Ferry, one of Nashville's two remaining ferries in operation, between Charlotte Avenue and Old Hickory Blvd. Cross the Cumberland in style.

*Enjoy a crafts demonstration at Ft. Nashborough.

*Attend a performance by the Children's Theatre, a chamber music concert or crafts shows in Centennial Park gratis of the Metro Board of Parks. Call for a list of summer events and schedules.

*Visit the Upper Room.

*Browse through Elder's Bookstore on Elliston Place. Stacks and shelves of new and old books. (It's fascinating.)

*Celebrate the 4th of July with free watermelon, Cokes and fireworks compliments of WSM-TV at Centennial Park.

*Tour the Governor's Residence by appointment Tuesdays and Thursdays 1 - 3 p.m. (Minnie Pearl lives next door!)

*Feed the ducks in Centennial or Shelby Park.

*Explore Music Row on foot. (See our highlights of the area.)

*Visit the Parthenon, the world's only replica of the original one in Athens.

*Attend church service at one of Nashville's beautiful old churches. Tulip Street Methodist, First Presbyterian Downtown or others listed in the back of this book.

*Jog through Centennial Park.

*Enjoy a free guided tour of the Tennessee State Capitol and a bird's eye view of the city.

*Play a game of tennis at one of the free municipal courts or at one of the area high schools.

*Take in the annual Iroquois Steeplechase.

*Visit Farmer's Market for a bit of local color.

*Window shop. There are hundreds of stores and at least six large malls or shopping centers in town.

*Trace your roots. Start with the Nashville Room of the Public Library and try the Tennessee State Library and Archives.

*Go hiking, bird watching, rock hunting or wild flower gathering at Percy Warner Park or Radnor Lake.

*Enjoy a free concert by the Nashville Symphony during the summer concert series in Centennial Park.

*Talk to the mynah birds and parrots for a few minutes at Jones Pet Shop in Hillsboro Village. It just might be the most interesting conversation you have had all year. (Great repertoire!)

*Walk slowly through the Arcade and let the special feeling of that old Nashville landmark sweep over you.

*Browse through the Nashville Flea Market. 450 exhibitors from 20 states gather here the last weekend of every month.

*Take one of Historic Nashville's great walking tours.

*Visit the old City Cemetery. William Driver, who coined the phrase "Old Glory" referring to the American flag, is buried there among others.

*Sunbathe and picnic at Old Hickory or Percy Priest Lake.

*Tour Lower Broad, Tootsie's Orchid Lounge, the Alamo, Ernest Tubb's Record Shop and absorb the nostalgia and color of this wonderful little area. It is gaudy but real.

*Attend the free "Midnight Jamboree," a continuation of the Grand Ole Opry broadcast live from Ernest Tubb's Record Shop. The midnight show features Grand Ole Opry stars and is broadcast every Saturday night after the Opry goes off the air.

*Walk through the Japanese Garden at Centennial Park during the spring. It is ablaze with tulips, jonquils, dogwoods, redbuds and azaleas.

*Take in a couple of local league baseball games at Shelby Park.

*Let the kids enjoy a free puppet show every Saturday at the Metro Public Library downtown. There're also a few fuzzy critters (live and adorable) to pet.

*Browse through the Tennessee State Museum. See a 3,000-year-old Egyptian mummy and much, much more.

*Attend a Nashville TV taping or a daily broadcast of the "Noon Show" on WSM. Become part of the audience for "Candid Camera," "The Porter Waggoner Show" or any number of other television specials. Call Opryland Productions for schedules and details as well as WTVF.

*Park by one of Nashville's lakes, turn off the motor, listen to the crickets and katydids, flip on WPLN and enjoy a mellow mood for an evening. Bring along a best friend and just talk; or watch the lights of fishermen on the lake; or a falling star if you are lucky.

*Bicycle through parts of Percy Warner Park.

*See the beautiful Ben Shahn mosaic at Peabody or the African art collection at at Fisk.

*Take in a free polo or soccer match. Polo is played at Percy Warner Park on the Highway 100 side and soccer is played next to Baird-Ward Pringting at the corner of Powell Avenue and Thompson Lane across from 100 Oaks Shopping Mall or call Vanderbilt for their season schedule.

*Enjoy free entertainment at lunch time compliments of the "Noon Time" program sponsored by First American Bank. Outdoors at its downtown headquarters during the summer.

*Tour the Ellington Agricultural Center. Old farm tools on display and a cool breeze always seems to lift the spirit. Nice landscape in autumn, too.

*Reserve Sycamore Lodge in Shelby Park or cook site in Percy Warner and whip up breakfast over an open fire one fine Sunday morning.

*Fly your kite in front of the Parthenon or over the waters at Old Hickory Lake from the shore or dam.

*Explore Edgefield, one of Nashville's oldest residential areas being restored.

*Wade in a creek on a hot summer day.

*Tour a Nashville industry. The Baptist Sunday School Board offers free tours as do others.

*If you haven't visited the Atlanta Hyatt Regency, take in the local Hyatt in Nashville. It is a copy of the famous Peachtree version. Ride one of its elevators and make plans to treat yourself to a night away from home soon.

*Take in some of the free art galleries at Vanderbilt, Peabody and Fisk. There are various exhibits there and throughout Nashville each year. Check the newspapers for listings and events.

*Request dates for free recitals and concerts from Blair Academy and Peabody College. Check the activities of such groups as the Friends of Chamber Music and the Nashville Pro Musica.

*Also take in Vanderbilt's free annual jazz concert in April.

*Attend the annual Tennessee Crafts Fair in Centennial Park in May.

*Star gaze and ferret out the home of your favorite country music artist. All the major tour companies offer guides to the homes of the stars, but here are our free directions to three of those homes:

JOHNNY CASH — go straight out Gallatin Road (or take the interstate north to Louisville and get off at the Two Mile Pike exit and follow Gallatin Road out past Hendersonville.) The House of Cash studio is just on the other side of Hendersonville. Take the Saundersville Access Road on the right, a real country lane, and bear to the left as it hugs the lake. Then there's June and Johnny's house, surrounded by a stone fence and fronting on the lake. WEBB PIERCE — out Franklin Road to North Curtiswood Lane. It's a rambling Tudor home on the corner. (The Governor's Mansion is on South Curtiswood Lane and Minnie Pearl lives next door.) ROY ACUFF — again out Gallatin Road to Ardee in Inglewood. Then Riverside Drive toward the old ferry, then right on Moss Rose, it's at 3940. A big, comfortable looking home with a flag pole in the front yard.

*View the original Tennessee art work which decorates the lobby of the Opryland Hotel.

*Meanwhile, there are free street fairs and parades at different times throughout the year in Nashville. There are the Elliston, Bandywood and Market street fairs; the Christmas, Easter and Veterans' Day parades.

*And don't forget there are dozens of free state or TVA parks nearby. Take an afternoon and visit the mysterious ancient walled structure at the Old Stone Fort in Manchester or see the highest waterfall east of the Rockies at Fall Creek Falls. Visit some historic Civil War battlefields or camp overnight at one of the free state parks.

*Then, if the spirit moves you, hit the road again and visit the Jack Daniel's and George Dickel distilleries about 70 miles south of Nashville. There are free tours and you'll really enjoy it! No admission charge.

Almost Free

*View Nashville from 364 feet in the air atop the Life and Casualty observation deck (see rain and snow fall upwards because of wind currents and down drafts). Adults 35 cents, children (under 12) 25 cents.

*Enjoy an amusement ride at Fair Park. Rides: 30 cents apiece.

*Consider playing golf at one of the public golf courses. Fee: $2.50 per nine holes.

*Buy a $3.30 license for three days and go fishing.

Rent A Building

Got a special event coming up? A surprise party, anniversary or reunion. Then why not rent a building?

It can be a once-in-a-lifetime remembrance. Diamond Jim Brady style. For example, the War Memorial Auditorium rents for only $250 per night. And then there's the Municipal Auditorium or the Grand Ole Opry House itself. Call the individual establishment for costs and details as well as availability.

SHOPPING

Department Stores

CAIN SLOAN
Downtown / 501 Church
Green Hills Village / 3855 Hillsboro Road
Rivergate Mall / Goodlettsville

CASTNER KNOTT
Donelson Plaza
Downtown / 618 Church
Green Hills Village / Hillsboro Road
Harding Mall / 4038 Nolensville Road
Rivergate Mall / Goodlettsville

HARVEY'S
100 Oaks Shopping Mall
Downtown / 518 Church
Madison Square Shopping Center / Gallatin Road

McCLURE'S
Harpeth Plaza / Highway 100
Hillsboro Village / 21st Ave. S.

Shopping Malls

Rivergate / Goodlettsville
100 Oaks / off Franklin Road
Green Hills / (shopping center) / Hillsboro Road
Belle Meade / (shopping center) / Harding Road

Special Shopping Streets and Areas

Elliston Place
Bandywood
Bavarian Village / Green Hills
Hillsboro Village
Carter's Court / Franklin
Third Ave. and Lower Broad / Downtown
The Arcade / Downtown
Farmer's Market / (fresh produce sold outdoors) / Downtown
Nashville Flea Market / (last weekend of every month) / State Fairgrounds

Women's Shops

GUS MAYER / Green Hills Shopping Center / 383-4771
GRACE'S / Harding Road near Belle Meade Shopping Center / 385-1160
LILLIE RUBIN / 100 Oaks / 292-3396

Nine Great Boutiques

N.Y. N.Y. / Bavarian Village / Green Hills / 292-7652
GALA / Carter's Court / Franklin / 790-0242
CASUAL CORNER / (3 locations)
CIAO / Green Hills / (Italian imports and accessories) / 297-7032
JAMIE'S / 117-L Stadium Drive / Hendersonville / (a super little shop) / 834-9525
PAUL HARRIS / Rivergate / 859-3330
UPS N DOWNS / Rivergate / 859-2861
COTTON PATCH / 100 Oaks / 385-3286

Call to make sure these are open before you go. All are very, very good.

Men's Shops

LEVY'S / 3 locations
HOLZAPHEL / Belle Meade Shopping Center / 383-0365
OXFORD SHOP / 2348 West End / 327-1220
BENNETT HOUSE / Franklin, Tennessee / 794-0506

Unusual Specialty Shops

MICHAEL CORZINE / Green Hills Shopping Center / 385-0140

BURRUS HARDWARE CO. / Green Hills Shopping Mall / (it's more than the name implies – great accessories and gifts) / 383-9722

TULIP TREE / 5423 Highway 100 / (beautiful flowers and accessories) / 352-1466

BRAZIL CONTEMPO / 2106 Crestmoor / Green Hills / (leather furniture) / 383-8330

HEARTH & PATIO / two locations / 3900 Hillsboro Road / 756 Two Mile Pike, Goodlettsville / (exactly what the name implies)

BED N' BATH / 3900 Hillsboro Road / (linens) / 269-5368

LAMP GALERIE / 4004 Hillsboro Road / (lamps, fixtures, accessories) / 383-8030

GOODIES / 200 2nd Ave. N. / (art, crafts, handmake items and more fills this historic old warehouse on Second Ave.) / 254-9697

GAMES STORE / 100 Oaks and Green Hills / (toys)

COOK'S NOOK / Bavarian Village / 383-5492

Antiques

Check the yellow pages in the telephone book. There are numerous shops scattered throughout Nashville. They range from nooks like *Betty Boops* on Elliston Place which sells antique clothes to *Elder's Bookstore* (old books, maps, out of print editions) to *Evelyn Anderson* which sells fine 18th and 19th century English and French pieces. Other recommended shops include *Bee Gee General Store, Brown's Antiques, Farmhouse, Jac's Gallery, Temptation Gallery,* and *Cecilia Binkley's.*

Visit the local antique malls, too. Green Hills and Hermitage. Also explore the malls in Murfreesboro and Lebanon. Franklin also offers *Pebblestone Court* and *Merritt House.* And don't forget the *Nashville Flea Market* which takes place the last weekend of every month at the State Fairgrounds. Admission: free. 450 exhibitors from 20 states selling everything imaginable under the sun.

Carter's Court in Franklin

Furniture Stores

Distinctive:
BRADFORD / 4100 Hillsboro Road / 297-3541
PERCY COHEN / 168 3rd Ave. N. / 255-7683

Discount:
MANUFACTURER'S WAREHOUSE / 9 Cumming Station / 255-4554
TARKINGTON SHOWROOM / 100 Powell Ave. / 385-3845
MORRIS FURNITURE WAREHOUSE / 7119 Centennial Blvd. / 298-4466
STOREHOUSE / 4105 Hillsboro Rd. / 385-0812

Explore:
Third Ave. S. downtown and Lower Broad for other furniture buys.
Associated Salvage for great fabrics and Williams Salvage for lamps, mirrors and more.

Imports:
PIER ONE / 2210 Crestmoor / Green Hills / 383-7184
HOUSE OF BAMBOO / 2 locations / 21st Ave. S. and Green Hills
WORLD BAZAAR / 2 locations / 100 Oaks and Rivergate Mall

Bargains In Them Thar Hills and Where to Find Them
(Factory outlets, discount stores and more up to 50% off)

Nashville Clothing

GENESCO COMMISSARY / 407 Woodland / Shoes, clothing, lingerie, brand name products, for men and women and children, good savings and terrific buys seasonally / 367-6401

WASHINGTON MANUFACTURING OUTLETS / six locations / Dee Cee brand jeans, painter's pants, tops, blouses, shirts, for men, women and teenagers.

MAY HOSIERY MILL / 425 Chestnut St. / Lingerie, men and children's socks and hose / 242-1615

BLUE BELL APPAREL FACTORY OUTLET / 948 Woodland / Jeans and more / 226-2433

FRIEDMAN'S ARMY-NAVY SURPLUS STORE / 3 locations / Jeans, sporting goods and army-navy wear as the name implies for men, women and teenagers.

BARGAIN BOUTIQUE / Bavarian Village / Green Hills / High fashion, designer clothes, are recycled here and sold on consignment basis. Evening gowns, suites, coats, skirts and leisure wear — all pre-owned women's clothing of exceptional quality and style at tremendous savings / 297-7900

Shoes

LOTTIES / 2 locations / Men and women's. Good looking shoes at discount savings.

UTOPIA BARGAIN SHOE STORE / 2140 Utopia Ave. / Boots can be bought here during the winter at great savings / 242-3851

GENESCO COMMISSARY / 407 Woodland / You name the famous brands and you'll probably find them right here / 367-6401

Brand Name Products — Watches, Camera, Jewelry, Appliances and more:

SERVICE MERCHANDISE / 2 locations / Great savings can be had here on just about anything. Nashville is the home of this multi-state company. Flip through their thick catalogue and enjoy the savings on 1000s of items.

Furniture

UNPAINTED FURNITURE CO. / 5526 Charlotte / 352-5229
WILLIAMS SALVAGE / 127 3rd Ave. S. / 256-6636
SALVATION ARMY / 5 locations
GOODWILL / 4 locations
MORRIS WAREHOUSE / 7119 Centennial Blvd. / 298-4466
MANUFACTURER'S WAREHOUSE / 9 Cummins Station / 255-4554
TARKINGTON SHOWROOM / 100 Powell Ave. / 385-3845

Also check the bargain bays at Bradford's, Percy Cohen and Payne furniture stores.

Miscellaneous

ASSOCIATED SALVAGE / 121 3rd Ave. N. / Fabrics, rugs and more / 255-2707

SPORTSMAN'S DISCOUNT / 2100 Greenwood / Complete line of hunting, fishing and archery supplies at discount prices / 228-0053

ROBERT ORR'S CASH AND CARRY / 1000 5th Ave. N. / Discounts on all kinds of food products for fancy parties or for large families / 254-1349

Out-of-town Outlets

WHITE STAG / Murfreesboro / Great savings on men and women's clothes. Name brands / 896-1233

FORMFIT ROGERS / Gallatin / Fabulous lingerie for women / 452-9939

ACME BOOTS / Clarksville / 552-2000

Action Auction

Finally, don't forget to tune in to WDCN's annual Action Auction in April. Hundreds of items from dinners with Grand Ole Opry stars to trips and paintings are auctioned off during this drive to raise money for the public television station.

SIDE TRIPS AND WEEKEND ESCAPES

If you are visiting Nashville, consider making it a base of operations for sorties, excursions, into the surrounding countryside. Here are a couple of outlined trips into Middle Tennessee, Alabama, Georgia and Kentucky. These are also terrific weekend escape ideas for Nashvillians. Pick up a map and enjoy:

The Southern Swing

Jack Daniel's Distillery — 70 miles south of Nashville in Lynchburg. The oldest registered distillery in the U.S. A must see. Free admission. Closed Thanksgiving, Christmas and New Year's. Plant closed on weekends but inquire about purchasing a barrel (good to use as a flower planter or halved as TV chairs, end tables or just a conversation piece). Sign the register, pick up a free postcard or two and enjoy. Also pick up a Jack Daniel's brochure and explore the hamlet of Lynchburg itself.
Visit the Lynchburg Ladies Handiwork Store, featuring handmade items — colorful quilts and crocheted afghans, the Hardware and General Store, the White Rabbit Saloon (sorry, Moore County is dry), the Drug Store with an old marble soda fountain and inquire at Mrs. Bobo Boarding House about an invitation to dinner. (I-24 South exit at Manchester to Lynchburg north on Hwy. 55. Distillery open 8-3:30 p.m.)

George Dickel Distillery — 70 miles south in Tullahoma. Not as old as Jack Daniel's but the General Store is a treat and Miss Annie's recipes for country cooking are great. Tour the distillery. Also drive by the nearby Normandy Dam — on a clear sunny day it is the most beautiful countryside in the world. Free admission to distillery. (I-24 south exit at Manchester.)

Tennessee Walking Horse Country — Shelbyville just up the highway from Tullahoma is home for the famed, world championship Tennessee Walking Horse Celebration held in August every year. Check the scenery: rolling pastures, white rail fences, big farms. Before country music, Middle Tennessee was first famous for its prized livestock, horses, mules and dark-fired tobacco. (I-24 south exit at Shelbyville/Bell Buckle Hwy. 231).

Sewanee — the area around Monteagle Mountain toward Chattanooga is an old time favorite escape for Nashville aristocracy who want to breathe fresh air and enjoy the majestic view from this "off the beaten path" hamlet. Monteagle brings to mind other resorts of yesterday: Beersheba and Hot Boiling Springs, fashionable oases when homes were un-airconditioned The elite University of the South is located in Sewanee, very Episcopal and picturesque. And during the summer they have a fine series of music concerts at the college. Also the Appletree Dinner Theatre is located in nearby Cowan. The renovated church building is owned by Nashville's Tupper Saussy. (I-24 South)

Chattanooga Choo-Choo

Lookout Mountain/Chattanooga — a full 2 to 2½ hour drive (and a time change from CST to EST) but if you have the time, it is worth it. The mountain itself is great, especially the "incline" trip up the hill; the houses range from summer cottages to palatial estates. There's Ruby Falls and Rock City; and the Chattanooga Choo Choo is absolutely marvelous. The old train station in Chattanooga has been renovated and turned into a great dining place for tourists (there are also great souvenirs here, too) and there is a Hilton motel in the rear of the complex. You can spend the night there or in one of the elegantly refurbished train cars. Voila: a taste of a by-gone era! (I-24 South)

All Aboard!

The proposed re-routing of the Amtrak *Floridian* in 1979 with stops in Nashville, Murfreesboro, Tullahoma and Chattanooga may open up new travel opportunities for those interested in train travel and riding the rails.

The new routing means that travelers can board the south-bound train in Nashville and stop off in any of the towns along the way, tour the local sights and then hop a north-bound train home.

The towns all boast some interesting attractions. Murfreesboro is a well-known antique center and there's historic Oaklands, an unusual rococo revival home, and the Stones River National Battlefield, 3 miles northwest of the city. There is also a White Stag factory outlet which offers great bargains for men and women.

Tullahoma is the home of George Dickel Distillery and nearby is Lynchburg, Jack Daniel's country. And, of course, Chattanooga is famous for Lookout Mountain, the incline and the beautifully restored Chattanooga Choo Choo, the old railroad station.

Check with Amtrak for details, schedules and cost. The *Floridian* originates in Chicago and its final destination is Miami.

Stones River National Battlefield, Sam Davis Home and Oaklands — ready to return to Nashville now? These stops along the way are optional. Interesting if you are a history or Civil War buff. Did you know there were more Civil War battles fought in Tennessee than in any other state, except Virginia? The Battle of Stones River was one of the bloodiest, at Oaklands Nathan Bedford Forrest accepted the surrender of Union forces in an 1862 victory and the home of Sam Davis is a memorial to the young man who was captured and hanged as a spy by Yankee forces. Murfreesboro is an antique lover's dream, too! (I-24 South at Murfreesboro)

Atlanta — Shop at Sak's, breakfast at Brennan's, saunter through Underground Atlanta. Or just spend an afternoon with the Braves or Falcons. Sprawling and hustling, Atlanta is jammed with sophisticated oddities. Like the Omni International and Peachtree Plaza hotels, Neiman-Marcus, Lanvin, Pucci, Rive Gauche, Charles Jourdan Valentino and Hermes shops, and scores of unusual restaurants — Max's, Mimi, Nikolai's Roof, Midnight Sun and Aunt Fanny's Cabin, among others. If Margaret Mitchell could just see her town now! It's a good four to five hours drive. Also nearby: Calloway Gardens, Six Flags Over Georgia and Warm Springs.

Atlanta Braves and sculpture on Peachtree

154

Shakertown at Pleasantville, Ky.

The Northern Swing: Kentucky

Hodgenville — the birthplace of Abraham Lincoln is the first stop off on this trip. The Sinking Springs Farm is interesting and the old oak tree looks like something out of your dreams. Decaying and majestic.

Bardstown — make sure to visit the old Talbot Inn, have lunch or dinner there and visit the brick mansion in Bardstown where Stephen Foster wrote "My Old Kentucky Home." Check out the distilleries, too. This is mint julep and Kentucky bourbon country. Also stop off at the nearby Trappist Monastery. Bring along some bread, a bottle of wine and some cheese and have a picnic in the meadow. Attend Vesper services in the evening. (P.S. women are not allowed in the monastery, except in the choir loft.)

Pleasant Hill (Shakertown) — the current hippie commune in Tennessee, Stephen Gaskin's Farm, has attracted widespread media attention, but this simple and extinct Shakertown village deserves the history or antique lover's attention. The Shakers were an odd outgrowth of the Quaker religion which flourished in the 19th Century. The intriguing communal movement is now almost non-existant, but the craftsmanship of these people live on in the 27 buildings located here. You can spend the night in one of the renovated living quarters, sleep in a high four poster bed in a room filled with quaint furnishings, rag rugs, wide plank flooring and a fireplace. Very reasonable and a memorable stay. Or just lunch or dine at the Trustee House Restaurant. Delicious food. Reservations a must.

Harrodsburg — on the way back look around this town. It was the first white settlement in Kentucky, founded by Daniel Boone.

Mammoth Cave — then heading home to Nashville stop off and visit this incredible cave. It runs for miles and miles and even on a torrid, hot summer day it is cool and refreshing. But for the adventuresome and hearty!

Got a Long Weekend?

Consider hopping a plane to Savannah, Ga., or Hilton Head, S.C. Or pack the kids into the car and head for Panama City. National holidays frequently give you a Monday tacked on to a weekend and, if you add an extra day or two, perhaps a Friday or Tuesday, from your vacation time, you get a long five-day vacation to unwind and break away from the tensions of the day. And, of course, there are hundreds of other ways to spend those days. Fishing, sleeping . . .

Note: Travel agencies are now beginning to offer special five-day holiday packages. Check out local offerings.

Short Jaunts

Franklin — a lovely little Southern town. Very genteel. Lots of restored homes and good shops at Carter's Court with its cobblestone courts, fountain, ferns, gas lights and very charming restaurant: Miss Daisey's Tea Room. There's also a Battle-Rama in the loft. Franklin is steeped in Civil War lore. (South on I-65)

Columbia — James K. Polk's ancestral home is located here. It contains furniture, silver, china and other relics used by the Polks in the White House. A National Historic Landmark. (South on I-65, 45 miles south of Nashville)

Huntsville, Alabama — home of the Alabama Space and Rocket Center and the NASA Marshall Space Flight Center. Interesting and a very pleasant drive. Space vehicles, moon rovers, rockets, space suits and more makes this attraction one of the largest space museums in the world. (Go I-65 south toward Birmingham)

Oak Ridge — close to Knoxville. The birthplace of modern atomic energy and the home of the Museum of Atomic Energy. This "atomic city" was built by the federal government during World War II and played an important role in the government's famous "Manhattan Project." (Go I-40 east)

Rugby — doomed Utopia. The last organized English colony in the U.S. In 1880 this settlement was founded to provide a pleasurable life for the younger sons of English gentry who by law were denied inheritance (1st born were anointed) and by custom forbidden to enter a manual trade. At one time 450 colonists lived here but typhoid, hard work (not a forte of dashing young men) and the burning of the Tabbard Inn (alas no ale) hastened the decline of this idyllic little village. 17 of the original 65 buildings remain. (State route 52, 17 miles east of Jamestown. Open March-November, Mon-Sat 10-5 p.m., Sun. 1-5 p.m. Closed Mon. Admission: $1.50)

Jamestown — south of this hamlet is the small town of Pall Mall where Alvin York lived. One of Tennessee's legendary heroes, he led seven men to capture 132 prisoners and killed 25 German soldiers in the process during the Battle of the Argonne Forest in WWI. He was awarded the Congressional Medal of Honor and Gen. Pershing called him the greatest hero of the war. See his farm and gristmill. (Hwy. 28 south of Jamestown. Open Sun-Mon 8-6 p.m.)

Presidential Route

There's Andy and James and Jefferson and Franklin and Jimmy. All just smiling down on you urging you to motor on down from Nashville to Plains, Ga., along the *Presidential Route* as they call it.

The route, I-65 to Montgomery and across on 85; U.S. 80 to Columbus, Ga., and U.S. 280 will lead you past some of America's great historic sites . . . the Hermitage of Andrew Jackson in Nashville, James K. Polk's home in Columbia, Tn., the White House of the Confederacy of Jefferson Davis in Montgomery, Franklin Roosevelt's Warm Spring, Ga., estate and then Plains, the home of Jimmy Carter.

Potpourri Travel Ideas

SCENIC DRIVE

Natchez Trace: Spanish moss, lush vegetation, cypress swamps, forests, creeks, and nature trails. No billboards or commercial trucks allowed. Slow down, turn off your CB radio and enjoy the scenery along this federal parkway between Natchez and Nashville (a link to Nashville remains to be completed). 450 miles of history. It was first an animal trail, then an Indian pathway and finally a wilderness road for pioneers. It is considered to be one of the most beautiful drives in America. (The Tennessee section begins at Tn. Hwy. 99 between Columbia and Hohenwald near Gordonsburg.)

GREAT SMOKY MOUNTAINS

Knoxville and Gatlinburg: Entry way into the most visited national park in the United States. *"Don't feed the bears"* signs don't stop critters with the munchies and the sight queque autos up for miles along these twisting mountain roads. Visit Clingman's Dome. Gatlinburg is a tourist trap (the traffic is ridiculous) but the Burning Bush Restaurant is a treat as are the mountains, crafts and scenery. There is skiing in the winter and lots of chalets. Also, there is a great Hyatt Regency in Knoxville. UT football games and Big Orange fans are indescribable! (I-40 East)

Rugby

Smoky Mountains and skiing in Gatlinburg

GRIST MILLS

Readyville Mill: Original mill was established in 1812. Flour and meal are ground here every day. (Admission: free. Take Highway 70 S and it is 12 miles east of Murfreesboro. Mon.-Sat. 9-5, Sun. 1-5.)

Falls Mill: A century old mill in Franklin County. Beautiful year round. Visit, picnic and just wander around. (Admission: free. Off highway 64 about 10 miles west of Winchester at Old Salem Crossroads.)

Alvin York's Farm and Grist Mill: This is where the legendary Alvin York was born and spent his life. (Free admission. On highway 28 south of Jamestown.)

U.T.'s Neyland Stadium in Knoxville

Civil War Shrines and Battlefields

Chickamauga: This national military park in Chattanooga is the nation's oldest, largest and most visited. For the number of men committed, it was the bloodiest battle in American history. The Confederate forces were ultimately forced to evacuate when Federal forces took Missionary Ridge opening the way to Atlanta and the "march to the sea." (I-24 south)

National Cemetery and Confederate Cemetery: The largest and most beautiful in the South. Both located in Chattanooga. (I-24 south)

Stones River National Military Park: Near Murfreesboro, this park was the site of another hard fought battle. Losses on both sides were very high: 12,000 confederate casualties and 13,000 Union casualties. (I-24 South)

Fort Donelson National Military Park: This was the scene of one of the first decisive battles of the Civil War. General Ulysses S. Grant commanded the Union forces at that time and the victory opened up the heart of the Confederacy to Union troops. (Off U.S. 79 West of Dover)

Shiloh National Military Park: This site contains a wealth of history for those really interested in the struggle between the North and South. It includes a well stocked Civil War Library, an exhibit room, maps of the battle and the war, a visitor center and a museum. (On Tennessee Highway 22 near Savannah, Tennessee.)

One of a Kind

Jonesboro: This is Tennessee's oldest town. It is 8 miles west of Johnson City in East Tennessee.

Andrew Johnson National Monument: Johnson is often the forgotten president from Tennessee. A native of Raleigh, North Carolina, he migrated to Greeneville, Tennessee in 1826 when he was 17 years old. He worked as a tailor and carved a career in politics. Unfortunately he was destined to succeed Abraham Lincoln and rule a war weary nation. Carpetbaggers and marshal law governed most of the South following the war and Johnson is the only American President against whom the House of Representatives approved impeachment proceedings. The memorial here includes his tailor shop, homestead and tomb. (Off Hwy. 11 E. in Greeneville.)

Davy Crockett Birthplace: Tennessee's most colorful native son. Humorist, bear hunter and hero in the Creek Indian War, he was also a state legislator, United States congressman and martyr in the cause for Texan independence. There are other Crockett memorials located throughout the state, including this one west of Johnson City, a tavern near Morristown and a state park northwest of Lawrenceburg. There is also a cabin displaying a rocking chair built by Crockett in Rutherford.

Greyhound races and Graceland Mansion;

Cordell Hull Birthplace: This is the memorial to the great statesman who worked to preserve peace and promote international understanding. (It is just a mile or so south of Byrdstown.)

Casey Jones Home: On April 30, 1900 at the throttle of "Old 382" at Vaughan, Mississippi, Casey Jones approached a stalled train on the same track. The brave engineer made an effort to slow the train and met his death. The only casualty of the wreck. As a result, he immediately became a legendary folk hero. Today the home of Casey Jones is maintained as a railroad museum in Jackson, Tennessee. (I-40 West)

Memphis Zoo    Graceland gates

Beale Street: Remember W. C. Handy? Beale street in Memphis is where blues was born. If you decide to visit the area, also take in the Overton Park Zoo in Memphis. And of course, there's the Pink Palace and the Mississippi River. There are shops and restaurants in Overton Square and good food to be found at Justine's and the Rendezvous (for the best ribs in town). Across the river in West Memphis, Arkansas, there are also dog races! And Elvis fans will want to visit Graceland Mansion. (I-40 West)

Kentucky Derby: Post time! The famous Churchill Downs plays host to this famous horse race the first Saturday in May every year. (Go I-65 North to Louisville, Kentucky.)

State Parks

Highest Waterfall East of the Rockies

Fall Creek Falls: It plunges 256 feet into a shaded pool. Gorges and chasms, timberland and a rustic but modern inn makes the 2nd largest park (16,000 acres) in Tennessee awfully popular. Other facilities: golf course, picnic and campgrounds, Olympic swimming pool and a playground. (State Highway 30 to Pikeville.)

Earthquake Born Wilds

Reelfoot Lake State Resort: This lake was formed by an earthquake in 1811. Resort inn and restaurant are built out over the lake amid the cypress trees. The partially submerged forest is a natural spawning ground for fish. Fishermen enjoy. Also scenic boat cruises. (West in the upper corner of the state, Highway 21)

Mysterious Ancient Walled Structure

Old Stone Fort Archaeological Area: The 1st white settlers were puzzled by this strange wall along the bluffs of the Duck River. It has been determined to have been built centuries before Christ. By Vikings, Indians or ??? (I-24 South exit Manchester U.S. 41)

Golfer's Paradise

Henry Horton State Park: Manicured tees and a resort inn. Swimming pools, horseback riding, skeet and trap range and lighted tennis courts make this a popular state park relatively close to Nashville. (I-65 North U.S. 31A)

Yachts to Sailboats

Paris Landing State Resort Park: Its full service marina is one of the largest and most modern in the state. Duck hunters use the inn in the winter. Other facilities: 18-hole golf course, lighted tennis courts, two swimming pools and camp sites. (Western part of the state. U.S. 79)

Mountain Laurel and Rhododendron

Roan Mountain State Resort Park: Hundreds of acres of beautiful rhododendron set this mountain ablaze during the summer. The annual Rhododendron Festival is in June. Picnic sites and camping areas are available. The Appalachian trail crosses this park. (Near the Tennessee/ North Carolina border. State Hwy. 143)

Square Dancing

Cedars of Lebanon State Day Use Park: Square dancing is featured every Saturday night at the recreation lodge. This particular park protects the largest remaining red cedar forest in the United States. Camp sites, picnic facilities and horse back riding. No inn. (I-40 East, U.S. 231 & Hwy. 10)

Reelfoot Lake

Indian Village

T.O. Fuller State Day Use Park: The historic Chucalissa Indian Village is located here. The village contains native houses, a historic temple, covered excavation and a museum. Park facilities also include golf course, picnic areas, swimming pool and campsites. (I-40 west near Memphis, U.S. 61)

Scenic Rivers

Hiwassee State Scenic River: This is the first designated state scenic river. It offers a wide variety of uses: canoeing, fishing, hiking and nature photography. Numerous launching ramps, picnic areas, and primitive camping sites. *(Also consider canoeing down the nearby Harpeth River. Also a scenic river.)* (Near Tn./N.C. border near Delano.)

Cannon Balls and Church Grounds

Montgomery Bell State Resort Park: Located within this park is the iron manufacturing operation which is said to have forged the cannon balls used by Andrew Jackson at the Battle of New Orleans. The park also contains the birthplace of the Cumberland Presbyterian Church. Facilities include an inn, restaurant, cabins, picnic areas, camp sites, horseback riding, boating, fishing, hiking trails and more. Close to Nashville. (Hwy. 70 West)

SPORTS BRIEF: FISHING, GOLF, TENNIS AND MUCH MORE

Sportsmen: Looking for an escape — a place to fish or nine holes of golf? A scenic river to canoe down or just a rustic campground? You are in luck. There are countless places to indulge your yearning for the outdoors.

"I kinda figure God must have made Tennessee first . . . while He was still fresh and full of good ideas." That's how the Tennessee Department of Tourism promotes the state's abundance of clear lakes, mountain streams, fields and meadows. And who is arguing?

Fishing and Boating

Two of the closest lakes in the Nashville area are Old Hickory (I-65 North) and Percy Priest (I-40 East). They are twenty minutes from downtown Nashville and offer marinas, boat ramps, and more. Bass, rockfish, walleye, catfish, and crappies are common varieties found in these area lakes. But note: residents and non-residents must carry a fishing license. They may be purchased for the day or longer and are available at most bait and tackle shops.

If you have the time, you might also want to try these other lakes in the Middle Tennessee area: Kentucky Lake (I-40 West), Center Hill Lake (I-40 East), Dale Hollow Lake (I-40 East), Cordell Hull Lake (I-40 East), Cheatham Lake (Hwy. 12 North).

For complete fishing details, pick up a Tennessee Department of Tourism brochure on the sport.

Golf

HARPETH HILLS / Old Hickory Blvd. off Hillsboro Road / 292-4558
   18 holes. Hours: Mon.-Fri. 8 a.m. til dark. Sat.-Sun. 5 a.m. til dark. $2.50 each nine holes.

SHELBY PARK / 20th & Russell (East Nashville) / 227-9816
   18 holes. Hours: Mon.-Fri. 8 a.m. til dark. Sat.-Sun. 7 a.m. til dark. Opens 6 a.m. in the summer. $2.50 each nine holes.

TWO RIVERS / Near Opryland / 889-9748
   18 holes. Mon.-Fri. 7 a.m. to 8 p.m. Sat.-Sun. 6 a.m.-8 p.m. Winter: Mon.-Fri. 8 a.m. til 5:30 p.m. Sat.-Sun. 7 a.m. til 5:30 p.m. $2.50 per nine holes.

McCABE / 40th and Murphy Road / 269-6951
   27 holes. Mon.-Fri. 7 a.m. til dark. Sat.-Sun. 6 a.m. til dark. $2.50 per nine holes.

Nashville Sounds

Tennis

Public Courts:

CENTENNIAL PARK / 75 cents per person, per hour / 327-9831
SHELBY PARK / (free) / 226-9211
AREA HIGH SCHOOL COURTS / free

Indoor:

TENNIS UNLIMITED / 3630 Redmon / 298-9247
RIVERGATE TENNIS / Two Mile Pike, Goodlettsville / 889-9006

Horseback Riding

WARNER PARK RIDING STABLES / Percy Warner Park / 352-4160
   Trained horses and riding trails. Reservations suggested on weekends and holidays. Fee: $4 per hour or 2-hour trail $7. Open 9 a.m. to 3:30 p.m. daily.

Sailing

Percy Priest and Old Hickory lakes are the closest.

Canoeing

The Harpeth, Duck and Buffalo rivers are all just an afternoon drive away.

Camping

There are scores of state parks in Tennessee. The closest to Nashville are Montgomery Bell, Cedars of Lebanon, and Henry Horton. See our separate listing of state parks and pick up a map of Tennessee for directions. A Tennessee Department of Tourism brochure also has additional information.

Hunting

Tennessee is alive with all kinds of small and wild game. There are duck and geese in migration; squirrel, rabbit, quail, dove and pheasant; deer and wild turkey in various areas and wild boar and black bear in East Tennessee. For further information on permits, regulations and seasons call or write: Tennessee Wildlife Resources Agency, P.O. Box 40747, Ellington Agricultural Center, Nashville, Tn. 37204 (741-1512).

Rentables

Breezed into town without the essentials? A sleeping bag, a tent or a canoe? Well, take heart. The Sportsman's Store, four locations, will rent sleeping gear, tents, back packs, and more, as will A-1 Morris Rent-All Centers, six locations. And the Buffalo Canoe Rental Co. in Flatwoods, Tn., near the Buffalo River will rent you a canoe.

Spectator Sports

NASHVILLE SOUNDS BASEBALL TEAM / Chestnut Street at Herschel Greer Stadium / Season: April til September. Game time 7:45 p.m. / Admission: $1-$3.25 / 242-4371.

NASHVILLE SPEEDWAY / Tennessee State Fairgrounds / Season: April to October every Saturday at 8 p.m. / Admission: $2-$16 / NASCAR sanctioned stock car racing / 242-4343

MUSIC CITY PRO CELEBRITY GOLF TOURNAMENT / Harpeth Hills Golf Course / Held every October usually the week before the Grand Ole Opry Anniversary Celebration / Call the Nashville Area Chamber of Commerce for details / 259-3900

IROQUOIS STEEPLECHASE / Percy Warner Park / Usually held in mid May / Admission: free / Thoroughbred races sponsored by the National Steeplechase and Hunt Association / Call the Nashville Area Chamber of Commerce for details / 259-3900

FRANKLIN RODEO / Franklin, Tennessee / Usually held the first week or two of May / Largest outdoor rodeo east of the Mississippi River. Bronco riding, calf roping and barrel racing / 794-1504

COLLEGIATE ATHLETICS / Football, baseball, basketball, track, tennis, soccer and more / Nashville's competitive collegiate teams take on rivals in various sports throughout the year / Check the local newspaper for times, schedules and games.

TENNESSEAN SAILING REGATTA / Old Hickory Lake / Held annually in April / Other sailing regattas are held in September and October and the Bluenose Regatta attracting top-notch competitors is held the first Saturday and Sunday in November / Call Jack Caldwell for details / 383-0347.

NICK GULAS NWA WRESTLING / Fairgrounds Arena / Every Wednesday night at 8 p.m. year-round / See professional wrestlers / Admission: Ring side $4 General admission Adults $3 Children under 10 years $2 / Televised locally / 297-9503

TENNESSEE WALKING HORSE CELEBRATION / Shelbyville, Tennessee / Usually held the last week of August / Internationally renown walking horse show / Call or write Tennessee Walking Horse National Celebration, Box 192, Shelbyville, Tenn. 37160 / 685-5915.

NASHVILLE AIR SHOW / Date varies but usually held mid August / Write or call Metro Nashville Airport Authority, Nashville, Tn. / 367-3029

Other Activities

MEMORIAL DAY OFFICIAL HANG GLIDING COMPETITION / Chattanooga / Newest attraction capturing the attention of outdoor sports enthusiasts /Call or write: Chattanooga Area Convention and Visitors Bureau, Memorial Auditorium, Chattanooga, Tn. 37402 / 266-5716

PARIS FISH FRY / Paris, Tennessee / Usually held toward the end of April / Fishing rodeo, parades and the "world's largest fish fry" / Write or call Paris Chamber of Commerce, P.O. Box 82, Paris, Tn. 38242 / (901) 646-3431

LIBERTY BOWL / Memphis / Usually the week before Christmas / Top seeded college teams play head on in this football classic / Call or write: 4272 Gwynne Road, Memphis, Tn. 38117 / (901) 767-7700

Nashville Speedway

Grab Bag

POLO / Games are played during the summer season near the Old Hickory Blvd. entrance to Percy Warner Park on Highway 100 S.

UNIVERSITY OF TENNESSEE / Knoxville / Watch the Big Orange take on Southeastern football rivals at Neyland Stadium / You ain't seen nothin' til you have seen Big Orange mania.

NASHVILLE BOAT DEALERS SHOW / Held every January / Displaying the latest in boats, equipment and more. Call the Municipal Auditorium for details.

GREAT LAKES OF THE SOUTH OUTDOOR SHOW / The South's largest sports show held in February at the Municipal Auditorium / Stage shows and entertainment plus equipment, boats, motors, camping gear and more / Call The Tennessean at 1100 Broad for details / 255-1221

KENTUCKY DERBY / Post time! The famous Churchill Downs plays host to this famous horse race the first Saturday in May every year. (Go I-65 North to Louisville.)

ANNUAL EVENTS

Paris Fish Fry

Spring/Summer

March

RUGBY WALKING TOUR: Four historic buildings in this once Utopian village are open for tours. March 1 - November 30. Write or call: P.O. Box 8, Rugby, Tn. 37733. (615) 628-3441.

WEARIN OF THE GREEN: A wee bit of Irish doings, parades, contests, and more to celebrate St. Patrick's Day. Usually held a few days in advance. Write or call: Houston County Jaycees, P.O. Box 266, Erin, Tn. 37061.

April

MULE DAY: Mule shows, auctions, races and the coronation of the King mule. Also pulling contests. Columbia is the "Mule Capital of the World." Usually held very early in the month. Write or call: Columbia Chamber of Commerce, Columbia, Tn. 38401. (615) 388-2155.

OPRYLAND SEASON OPENS: Usually the weekend after Easter. Open only on weekends until June. Call or write: Opryland USA, P.O. Box 2138, Nashville, Tn. 37214. (615) 889-6600.

SOUTHEASTERN 500 RACE: Race car lovers enjoy! Held very early in the month. Call or write: Bristol International Speedway, Bristol, Tn. 37620. (615) 764-1161.

DOGWOOD ARTS FESTIVAL: The hills are abloom. And there are 58 miles of marked trails. Concerts, parades, arts and crafts shows. Usually held in mid-month when the dogwoods are in bloom. Write or call: P.O. Box 2229, Knoxville, Tn. 37901. (615) 637-4561.

EAST TENNESSEE STRAWBERRY FESTIVAL: Welcome spring with bluegrass music, a parade, square dancing, and, of course, a shortcake eating contest. This festival has been held annually for more than 30 years. Held toward the end of the month. Write or call: Dayton Chamber of Commerce, 305 E. Main Street, Dayton, Tn. 37321. (615) 775-0361.

PARIS FISH FRY: "The world's largest fish fry." With fishing rodeo, parades and more. Savor and enjoy! This annual event is held near Kentucky Lake. Write or call: Paris Chamber of Commerce, P.O. Box 82, Paris, Tn. 38242. (901) 646-3431.

Tennessee Crafts Fair at Centennial Park

May

TENNESSEE CRAFTS FAIR: Craftsmen from all over Tennessee exhibit their wares in front of the Parthenon in Centennial Park in Nashville. Pottery, leather work, quilts, batiks, baskets and much, much more. A must see! Usually held the first weekend in the month. Write or call: Nashville Area Chamber of Commerce, 161 4th Ave. N., Nashville, Tn. 27219. (615) 259-3900.

FRANKLIN RODEO: The largest outdoor rodeo east of the Mississippi. Bronco riding, calf roping and barrel racing. Usually held the first part of the month. Write or call: P.O. Box 609, Franklin, Tn. 37064. (615) 794-1504.

COTTON CARNIVAL: Parades, music and gala parties. All in honor of old "King Cotton." Usually held middle or late month. Call or write: Memphis Area Chamber of Commerce, 42 South Second Street, Memphis, Tennessee 38103.

MUSIC CITY USA 420 WINSTON CUP GRAND NATIONAL STOCK CAR RACE: Features some of the biggest names in official championship racing. Usually held mid month. Write or call: Nashville Speedway, P.O. Box 40048, Nashville, Tn. 37204. (615) 242-4343.

IROQUOIS STEEPLECHASE: Usually held mid-month. One of the oldest amateur steeplechases around. Thoroughbred races sponsored by the National Steeplechase and Hunt Association. A very popular event. Write or call: Nashville Area Chamber of Commerce, 161 4th Ave. N., Nashville, Tennessee 37219. (615) 259-3900.

KENTUCKY DERBY: Post time! The famous Churchill Downs plays host to this famous horse race the first Saturday in May every year. Call or write: Louisville Visitors and Convention Bureau.

MEMORIAL DAY HANG GLIDING COMPETITION: The newest attraction capturing the attention of scores of outdoor enthusiasts. Soar like a bird or watch others. Call or write: Chattanooga Area Convention and Visitors Bureau, Memorial Auditorium, Chattanooga, Tn. 37402. (615) 266-5716.

NASHVILLE SYMPHONY ORCHESTRA PARK CONCERTS: This is part of the Metro Summer Park Program. Beginning the end of this month. The summer program also includes performances by the Children's Theatre, Chamber Music concerts, crafts shows and more. All free. Call or write: Metro Board of Parks and Recreation, Centennial Park, Nashville, Tn. 37203. (615) 259-6400.

June

ANNUAL INTERNATIONAL COUNTRY MUSIC FAN FAIR: Paradise for the true-blue country music fan. A week of continuous entertainment — stage shows, concerts, picture and autograph sessions and more all for the fans. $30 registration fee. Usually held the first week or so of the month. Call or write: Fan Fair, P.O. Box 2138, Nashville, Tn. 37214. (615) 889-7503.

Fan Fair... a continuous round of shows and activities for the country music fan

GRANDMASTER'S FIDDLING CONTEST: At Opryland and open to all park guests. Held during Fan Fair week. Write or call: Opryland, Box 2138, Nashville, Tn. 37214. (615) 889-6600.

OAKLAND'S ASSOCIATION ANTIQUE SHOW AND SALE: Almost 25 years old, this show pulls dealers from across the country. Usually attracts about 45 dealers and is held mid month. Call or write: Oakland Mansion, Murfreesboro, Tn. 37130. (615) 893-0022.

RHODODENDRON FESTIVAL: 400 acres of blooming rhododendron atop Roan Mountain. Also includes several events, parade, crafts fair and more. Held 2nd or 3rd week of the month. Call or write: Box 311, Johnson City, Tn. 37601. (615) 543-2122.

July

"DOWN TO EARTH" ALL DAY GOSPEL SING: An old fashioned all day gospel sing. A vanishing bit of Americana. Go and enjoy. Held usually mid month. Call or write: Alexandria Lions Club, Alexandria, Tn. 37012.

UNIVERSITY OF THE SOUTH CONCERT SERIES: Escape the heat and confusion of the city to a cool, picturesque University of the South concert in Sewanee atop Monteagle Mountain. Concerts usually held on Sundays. About a 1½ hour drive. Write for further information: University of the South, Sewanee, Tn. Or check the newspaper for listings and times.

August

INTERNATIONAL BANANA FESTIVAL: South Fulton, Tennessee is at the crossroads of banana shipments from South America to points north. So, why not throw a festival in honor of the location? Bands from South America entertain, and parades, and carnivals make for a gala affair. Usually held mid month. Also country and western entertainment. And a famous one-ton banana pudding. Write or call: International Banana Festival, Inc., Box 428, South Fulton, Tn. (502) 472-2975.

TENNESSEE WALKING HORSE NATIONAL CELEBRATION: The finest walking horses from all over the world. Show has been held for more than 40 years. Usually held last part of the month. Write or call: Tennessee Walking Horse National Celebration, Box 192, Shelbyville, Tn. 37160. (615) 684-5915.

NASHVILLE AIR SHOW: Watch them soar and dive. A great end of the season event. Dates vary. Call or write: Metro Nashville Airport Authority, Nashville, Tn. (615) 367-3029.

Tennessee Walking Horse Celebration

Fall/Winter

Longhorn Rodeo

September

LONGHORN RODEO: Headquartered in Nashville, Longhorn is the world's largest producer of indoor rodeos. The local show is staged every Labor Day weekend at the Municipal Auditorium. Featuring professional big league bareback bronco riding, calf roping, saddle bronc riding, barrel racing, steer wrestling and bull riding. Call or write: Longhorn Rodeo, P. O. Box 8160, Nashville 37207. (615) 876-1016.

ITALIAN STREET FAIR: A family outing to benefit the Nashville Symphony. Booths and bargains, pasta and other foods and entertainment by the Symphony. Usually held early in the month. Call or write: Nashville Symphony Association, 1805 West End, Nashville, Tn. 37203. (615) 329-3033.

TENNESSEE STATE FAIR: Midway rides, stage shows, exhibits and more. Usually held mid month. Call or write: Tennessee State Fair, P.O. Box 40208, Nashville, Tn. 37204. (615) 254-3521.

October

NATIONAL QUARTET CONVENTION: Days of gospel music kick off this month of music in Nashville. Held usually the first week of the month. Call or write: National Quartet Convention, P.O. Box 23190, Nashville, Tn. 37202. (615) 256-1255.

MUSIC CITY PRO-CELEBRITY GOLF TOURNAMENT: Top pros and celebrities from music, movies and television get together for fun. Attracts a large gallery and is a popular event. Usually held the first week or so in the month. Call or write: Music City Pro-Celebrity Golf Tournament, c/o Richland Country Club, Elmington Ave., Nashville, Tn. 37205. (615) 292-6927.

ANNUAL ANNIVERSARY OF THE GRAND OLE OPRY: A celebration of the founding of this incredible radio program. It draws thousands into town for banquets, parties and the nationally televised County Music Association Awards Show. The entire music industry from Los Angeles to New York turns out for this local celebration. Usually held mid month. Call or write: Opryland, Box 2138, Nashville, Tn. 37214. (615) 889-6600.

AUTUMN LEAF SPECIAL TRAIN TRIP TO CROSSVILLE: Take a vintage steam engine train from Chattanooga for the five hour trip to Crossville and enjoy the gorgeous autumn scenery. Usually held around mid month. Call or write: Tennessee Valley Railroad Museum, Box 5263, Chattanooga, Tn. 37406. (615) 265-8861.

Trees of Christmas at Cheekwood

December

"TREES OF CHRISTMAS" EXHIBIT AT CHEEKWOOD: A beautiful exhibit of Christmas trees as decorated from around the world. A must see. Usually held from the second week of the month until a week before Christmas. Call or write: Fine Arts Center, Cheek Road, Nashville, Tn. 37205. (615) 352-5310.

LIBERTY BOWL: Top seeded college teams play head on in this football classic. Usually held the week before Christmas. Call or write: 4272 Gwynne Road, Memphis, Tn. 38117. (901) 767-7700.

January

NASHVILLE BOAT DEALERS SHOW: Displaying the latest in marine boats, equipment and more. Usually held mid month. Call the Municipal Auditorium for details.

February

LAWN AND GARDEN FAIR: Go to this event. It is wonderful. A breath of spring in the cold, dead of winter. See tulips, jonquils, forsythia and more abloom. Plants for sale and lectures as well as booths and displays. Usually held mid month. Call or write: Nashville Area Chamber of Commerce, 161 4th Ave. N., Nashville, Tn. 37219. (615) 259-3900.

GREAT LAKES OF THE SOUTH OUTDOOR SHOW: The South's largest sports show. Stage shows and entertainment and the latest in equipment, boats, motors, camping and more. Usually held mid month. Call or write: Tennessean, 1100 Broad, Nashville, Tn. 37203. (615) 255-1221.

VANDERBILT IMPACT SYMPOSIUM: Hear and see nationally prominent speakers address the issues of the day. Usually held mid month. Very interesting and attracts a sophisticated audience. Call or write Vanderbilt University for further details.

Tennessee State Fair

Note: There are, of course, scores of events not listed here. They include historic tours of homes and buildings, special events sponsored by local organizations such as the Symphony Outing or Swan Ball (which are private and rather expensive affairs for members), special exhibits and displays by individual civic clubs and community organizations. So please check the newspapers often for listings and news about various events.

WHAT'S LEFT

News Sources

For keeping up, check the newspapers' daily entertainment advertisements. The Tennessean offers a Sunday Showcase which includes a weekly roundup of movies, concerts and attractions. The Banner features a special Weekender section in its Thursday edition. The Tennessean carries a similar weekend rundown on Friday which includes announcements of the Grand Ole Opry lineup. The Tennessean also publishes a monthly magazine the first Sunday of every month which highlights mid-state events. And Nashville! magazine carries a monthly listing of activities and miscellany. All the above publications also carry interesting news stories on local history, events and activities.

Favorite Newsstands and Bookstores

Mill's / 21st Avenue South
Zibart's / Green Hills
Bookworld / (terrific magazine rack) / Church Street
Walden's / Rivergate

Beautiful Churches

DOWNTOWN PRESBYTERIAN CHURCH / 154 Fifth Ave. N. at Church St. / 254-7584
   An Egyptian revival church located on a historic site.

CHRIST CHURCH EPISCOPAL / 900 Broad / 255-7729
   Gargoyles and Tiffany windows adorn this circa 1892 church.

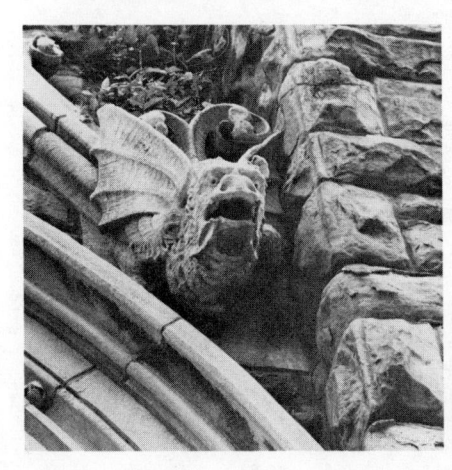

ST. MARY'S CATHOLIC CHURCH / 5th Ave. N. at Charlotte / 256-1704
    Built in 1845 by William Strickland. It was the first Catholic Church in Tennessee.

TULIP STREET UNITED METHODIST / 522 Russell St. / 255-6248
    This 1891 church in historic Edgefield is noted for its beautiful terra cotta facade.

Other Notable Places of Worship

MADISON CHURCH OF CHRIST / 106 Gallatin Road / 868-3360
    This church boasts one of the largest Sunday School classes in the world. Services are broadcast on local television and Minister Ira North is a powerful personality.

THE TEMPLE / 5015 Harding Rd. / 352-7620
    This Jewish synagogue is beautifully located in Belle Meade.

Note: There are at least 700 churches in Nashville. Check the telephone book for a complete listing or the register in your hotel or motel for the closest ones.

Tennessee Facts

Climate: Average Summer   76.4F
         Average Winter   40.4F
         Average Annual Rainfall   49.69 inches

Population: 4,188,000 (58.8% urban)

Largest Cities: Memphis, Nashville, Knoxville and Chattanooga

Nickname: Volunteer State . . . earned as a result of the number of volunteers furnished by the state to the War of 1812 and the Mexican War.

State Name: Tennessee is of unknown Cherokee origin. Early white men knew only that it referred to the name of a river and an ancient Cherokee capital.

State Flower: Iris
State Bird: Mockingbird
State Song: "Tennessee Waltz"
State Insect: Ladybug
State Tree: Tulip poplar

Helpful Phone Numbers

Emergency for fire, police or ambulance: 911

Weather: Traveler's Advisory 361-6416
Local Forecast 259-4111

Chamber of Commerce Tourist Information: 259-3900
and Hotel Room Finder Service: 244-8080

Tennessee Department of Tourism Information: 741-2158

Photo Credits:

Tennessee Department of Tourism; Tennessee Archives and Library; Country Music Association; Charles Warfield, Tennessee Historical Commission; Bill Lefevor Photography; Standard Candy Company; Tennessee Performing Arts Foundation; Hyatt Regency; George Baker, Chattanooga Times; Opryland USA; Country Music Hall of Fame and Museum; Lee Grisby, Metro Parks; Sailmaker Restaurant; RCA; Volunteer Jam, Sound Seventy; Julian's Restaurant; Nashville Symphony; Advent Theatre; Fisk University; Academy Theatre; Jack Shwab, Cheekwood; Carter's Court; Jack Daniel's Distillery; Atlanta Chamber of Commerce; Buckhorn Press; University of Tennessee; Memphis Chamber of Commerce; Nashville Speedway; Nashville Sounds; Vanderbilt University; Daniel Brown, Tennessee Artists and Craftsmen's Association; Tennessee Walking Horse Celebration; Tennessee State Fair; Bob Grannis Photography; Michael Baldridge Photography; Exit-In; and Dean Dixon Photography.